MAKING GOVERNMENTS PLAN

MAKING GOVERNMENTS PLAN

State Experiments in Managing Land Use

RAYMOND J. BURBY and PETER J. MAY

with

Philip R. Berke
Linda C. Dalton
Steven P. French
Edward J. Kaiser

The Johns Hopkins University Press
Baltimore and London

Published in cooperation with the Center for
American Places, Harrisonburg, Virginia

© 1997 The Johns Hopkins University Press
Printed in the United States of America on acid-free paper
06 05 04 03 02 01 00 99 98 97   5 4 3 2 1
The Johns Hopkins University Press
2715 North Charles Street, Baltimore, Maryland 21218-4319
The Johns Hopkins Press Ltd., London

Library of Congress Cataloging-in-Publication Data
will be found at the end of the book.
A catalog record for this book is available
from the British Library.

ISBN 0-8018-5623-X

Contents

Preface and Acknowledgments

The past fifty years have witnessed unprecedented changes in land use across the United States. Not content with its consequences, policy makers in state and local government have searched for tools to manage development. They have sought mechanisms that would bring about the benefits of growth while avoiding the environmental degradation, congestion, housing shortages, and other problems that often accompany rapid changes in land use. Invention has been the order of the day as uncounted new methods for coping with these changes have been tried. The growth management tool kit is filled with a seemingly endless array of techniques: timed development, growth boundaries, subdivision exactions, impact fees, linkage programs, moratoriums, visioning, ordinances regarding adequate facilities, tax increment financing, and fair share housing, to name only a few.

States also have experimented with different governmental arrangements for addressing improper development. Once reluctant partners with local governments in managing land use, a number of states have forged new systems of governance to link local policy more closely to state goals and standards and to cajole (and sometimes coerce) cooperation among neighboring localities. These are the lesser-studied but all-important aspects of the quiet evolution of land use policy.

One of the most important changes going on in development management today is the reinvigoration of planning. City plans are as old as cities in America, but plans have been under attack from a number of quarters. Public administrators, looking at the legacy of "paper" plans produced by the federal government's "701" planning assistance program, came to view them as irrelevant to sound public policy. Planning theorists, looking at the limitations of rational decision making, came to similar conclusions.

Some states, however, have not been content to let localities regulate development without their first thinking through the problems (and opportunities) development poses and without giving attention to the goals the states want to accomplish in the course of managing growth. By making local governments prepare comprehensive plans, these states have put plans and planning to a new test. Are the plans the states have demanded producing greater commitment and capacity to manage growth? Are plans resulting in more-intelligent use of growth management tools, more-extensive programs for growth management, and more-effective governmental intervention in urban growth processes than would occur in their absence?

These state planning requirements also test intergovernmental arrangements. Have these states done an adequate job of designing mandates and structuring their implementation so that local governments are persuaded to plan for, as well as manage, growth? Do they have in place the tools needed to build local capacity to plan? Have the states coordinated their various environmental and other regulatory programs so that they reinforce local planning and growth management?

These are important policy questions. But innovations in growth and development management have not been matched by a parallel increase in understanding of these issues. The need for plans has been debated hotly among planning academics, but the questions theorists raise have been answered more by conjecture than by facts. Little is known about the actual contribution that plans make to programs of local growth management. Similarly, the literature in intergovernmental relations and policy implementation is replete with competing theories about how to structure and effectuate intergovernmental programs, but most of those theories have never been systematically evaluated.

That is not to say there is lack of academic attention to these topics. The literature in growth management, intergovernmental relations, and policy implementation is full of descriptive case studies. Most of that work focuses on a single growth management tool, a single jurisdiction's experience with a growth problem, or implementation of a single program or espouses a single point of view. Virtually none of the case literature draws on and builds theory. As a result, policy learning has been slow.

With these considerations in mind, we undertook a systematic comparative study of the efforts states make to foster better management of urban growth. In this book, we present the findings and policy conclusions from our five-state comparative study of state planning mandates and their impacts on the development-management programs of local governments.

The book is unique in two ways. First, we consciously build a theory to explain the influence of state mandates on local plans and planning and to explain the combined impacts of these factors on local development management. Second, we examine that theory through use of a quasi-experimental research design that permits inferences about the effectiveness of state mandates and local plans. Three states with planning mandates of varying strength and sophistication are compared with two states without planning mandates. We examine experiences of local governments with plans of varying quality to see how planning has affected local management of development. This combination of theorizing and empirical testing through a large-scale field investigation is rare for research about planning or policy implementation.

This book has three parts. In part 1, we examine attempts by five states to cope with rapid growth through state planning mandates. For those who want to know more about state policy innovation and the alternative ways states have addressed development problems, these chapters provide a look in some depth at the evolution of the mandates. Chapter 2 focuses on California, which first mandated local planning in 1937 and over time expanded that mandate to cover a variety of issues of state concern. Chapter 3 examines North Carolina, whose 1974 coastal planning mandate is arguably the country's most successful coastal management program. Florida, whose program for growth management is described in chapter 4, was also in the vanguard of state planning, but the revisions in 1984 and 1985 to its earlier planning legislation have now made it the preeminent example of the second wave of state programs. Part 1 concludes with a look in chapter 5 at Texas and Washington. Until Washington policy makers enacted growth management legislation in 1990, these two states had not chosen comprehensive-planning requirements as a means for addressing land use problems. Instead, they relied on single-purpose mandates to address specific land use problems.

In the three chapters of part 2, we evaluate experiences of state and local governments with comprehensive-planning programs. Chapter 6 shows how differences in the way legislation is designed and in the state agencies assigned to carry out the policies affect policy implementation. These factors affect both the effort states devote to carrying out planning policies and the character of state agency dealings with local governments. Chapter 7 addresses the influence of state mandates on the quality of local governmental plans and the resulting commitment of local officials to state goals. We show that mandates play a critical role in the attention local plans give to state policy objectives. We also show that mandates and plans have some impact on the commitment of local officials to state goals. In chapter 8, we assess the relation between local plans and development management. We show that the quality of local plans affects the character of local development management. High-quality plans, when accompanied by strong commitment of local officials, steer localities toward more-comprehensive approaches toward development management.

In part 3, comprising a concluding chapter, we present the implications of our analyses of comprehensive state planning programs. We provide lessons for crafting more-effective state legislation and for implementing programs at both the state and local levels. We extend those findings to the federal government, which has tended to avoid land use planning as an approach to problems of national significance. We also identify gaps in our theorizing as a basis for further research.

To carry out the research, we put in place a collaborative network of scholars in each of the five states where primary data collection was to be undertaken. The team included Linda C. Dalton and Steven P. French at California Polytechnic State University; John M. DeGrove at Florida Atlantic University/Florida International University; Raymond J. Burby and Edward J. Kaiser at the University of North Carolina at Chapel Hill; Philip R. Berke at Texas A & M University; and Peter J. May at the University of Washington. The overall efforts of the research team were coordinated by the core research group at the University of North Carolina at Chapel Hill, which also maintained statistical data files provided by each institution. This collaborative approach made it possible for us to assemble a large database on state and local governments that could be analyzed using tools of statistical inference. Equally important, it also made it feasible to employ qualitative research methods through case studies and face-to-face interviews with officials in each of the states and jurisdictions we studied.

We think readers can put this book to several uses. For those interested in crafting effective intergovernmental policy and programs for the management of growth, the book provides an understanding of policy designs and growth management tools that are working well in state and local government. For scholars interested in intergovernmental relations, policy implementation, and planning theory, the book synthesizes and extends previous work and provides one of the few systematic empirical tests of various conceptualizations that have emerged over the past decade. For instructors in planning and political science, the book can be used in classes dealing with intergovernmental policy design and growth management. Finally, we think policy researchers will find this work an interesting example of the field network approach to data collection. Given present-day budgetary constraints, this may be the only feasible way to undertake large-scale collection of field data to test theories of governmental action.

The book is truly a collaborative effort of the research team led by Raymond J. Burby. Team members drafted different chapters, after which Burby and Peter J. May collaborated as lead authors in putting those words into a cohesive whole; they also collaborated in writing the introductory chapter. In addition, Burby took the lead in writing the four chapters in part 1 on state growth management programs; and collaborated, with Philip R. Berke and Steven P. French, on chapter 7, on enhancing planning, and, with Linda C. Dalton, on chapter 8, on managing development. May took the lead in writing chapter 6, which addresses the design and implementation of state mandates, and chapter 9, which puts forth suggestions for crafting more effective state programs for planning and managing development. Berke and French contributed to the development of chapter 7, which addresses the quality of local comprehensive plans. Berke also contributed to chapter 5, on planning and growth management in Texas. French also contributed to chapter 2, on planning and managing development in California. Dalton took the lead in the development of chapter 8, on managing development, and also contributed to chapter 2. Edward J. Kaiser contributed to the methodological appendix and provided material for chapter 1, on state growth management programs, chapter 3, on the North Carolina planning mandate, and chapter 7, on plan quality. John M. DeGrove and his colleagues at Florida Atlantic University/Florida International University, although not among the book's coauthors, contributed material to the chapters describing state growth management programs and over the four years the research was under way aided our interpretations of the field data.

A study of this scope could only be conducted with the help of a number of other persons. We are indebted to many research assistants who contributed to the data collection effort. In particular, we want to acknowledge the role of Dale Roenigk of the University of North Carolina at Chapel Hill, who coordinated assembly of the data and prepared the first drafts of the sections of the book dealing with the implementation of policies proposed in plans. We also deeply appreciate the dedicated work of M. Ellen Hickey at California Polytechnic State University; Craig Diamond and Susan Trevarthen at Florida Atlantic University/Florida International University; Andrée Jacques and Deborah Jackson at the University of New Orleans; Elisabeth S. Moore and Maureen A. Heraty at the University of North Carolina at Chapel Hill; Carla Prater at Texas A & M University; and Thomas A. Birkland and Nancy Stark at the University of Washington.

Earlier versions of various portions of this work were presented for critical discussion before a number of academic and professional forums. In addition, some of our findings have been published as articles in the *Journal of the American Planning Association*, the *Journal of Planning Education and Research*, the *Journal of Policy Analysis and Management*, *Publius: The Journal of Federalism*, and *Public Administration Review*. We learned much from the feedback we obtained from our conference presentations and from comments by reviewers about the journal articles. We also have learned much from the growing cohort of growth management scholars. Readers will see ideas here garnered from the work of, among others, Scott Bollens, Dennis Gale, David Godschalk, Robert Healy, Judith Innes, Gerrit Knaap, Thomas Pelham, and Frank Popper. We hope they find this contribution a worthy addition to this growing field of scholarship.

Finally, we would like to acknowledge the financial and other aid from the universities with which the research team was associated during this study: California Polytechnic State University (Dalton, French); Florida Atlantic University/Florida International University (DeGrove); Georgia Institute of Technology (French); the University of New Orleans (Burby); the University of North Carolina at Chapel Hill (Burby and Kaiser); Texas A & M University (Berke); and the University of Washington (May). We are also indebted to William A. Anderson, who served as National Science Foundation program manager for the study, and to the National Science Foundation, which supported this work through research grant no. BCS-8922346. Of course, the contents of this book are not necessarily endorsed by the National Science Foundation or those who shared their experiences and observations as part of our data collection and analysis.

MAKING GOVERNMENTS PLAN

1

The States and Planning Mandates

Land and its use. Ignored for decades on the national scene and relegated to the backwaters of local government management, land use has emerged as a critical yet frequently intractable issue. The reasons are not complex. Improper land use has been implicated in a host of problems, ranging from inner-city decay and traffic congestion to air, water, and other forms of environmental pollution. Productive land use is central to economic well-being, accounting for two-thirds of national wealth and one-sixth of personal income. Because land use invariably affects financial well-being, governmental decisions concerning development tend to be highly controversial—so much so that for decades state and national policy makers were content to leave land use regulation to the discretion of local governments.

That hands-off stance began to change in the early 1960s, when a so-called quiet revolution in state land use management was sparked by Hawaii's decision to centralize some of its land use regulation. The revolution gained momentum in the 1970s, when public opinion polls revealed substantial concern about environmental degradation and the negative consequences of urban growth. By the end of the decade, ten states (California, Colorado, Florida, Hawaii, Massachusetts, New Jersey, New York, North Carolina, Oregon, and Vermont) had adopted comprehensive land use management programs for application either statewide or to critical environmental areas. Thirty other states had adopted more narrowly conceived state regulatory programs for particularly sensitive environments such as wetlands and shorelines.

State efforts at land management reform briefly subsided in the early 1980s. By the mid-1980s, they gained new momentum. Legislation enacted since that time comprises the "second wave" of state land use management. Florida and Vermont substantially strengthened existing laws, and by 1992 new comprehensive programs had been adopted in Georgia, Maine, Maryland, Rhode Island, and Washington. In contrast with the strong environmental focus that characterized the first wave of land management legislation in the 1970s, the second wave has had more balanced aims with respect to managing growth and protecting the environment.

Common and Divergent Paths to Governing Land Use

Both the first and second waves of state land use management reforms have shared one central tenet: the need for greater centralization in decisions regarding land use. Reformers believe centralization will help to resolve land use and development problems that have noteworthy consequences for more than a single locality. States have taken two different but not mutually exclusive approaches to addressing these so-called issues of greater-than-local concern. One approach focuses on a single state objective to be achieved through state and local regulation. We refer to this as the single-purpose approach to governing land use and development. The other approach consists of a comprehensive state and local governmental planning process aimed at achieving a broad range of state policy objectives. We refer to this as the comprehensive-planning approach.

The Single-Purpose Approach

The single-purpose approach involves states preempting the authority of local governments over a single issue (e.g., the siting of a power plant) or a type of area (e.g., wetlands). States promulgate rules governing land use or development for the particular situation. Those rules are then imposed on the private sector either directly by the state or through enforcement actions taken by local governments. The single-purpose approach concentrates responsibilities for specifying relevant standards and the means for achieving them in state agencies. Local governments are expected to act as agents of the state in enforcing the state-designated rules rather than as fellow artisans in crafting state policy and its implementation.

This approach is based on a fundamental premise that local governments are unwilling or unable to address land use problems that have noteworthy regional impacts. According to this premise, local governments do not adequately consider the impacts beyond their political boundaries of major land use or development decisions. Observers such as Logan and Molotch (1987) characterize local governments as either unwilling to impose strict environmental standards or whipsawed by local industries into relaxing standards to an unacceptable degree. This view is also evident in various studies (National Commission on Urban Problems 1968; Rowe 1978; Jennings 1989) that portray local governments as dominated by parochial interests, overly responsive to local political pressures, and lacking in needed expertise to make wise decisions about land use. To the extent that these conditions exist, state policies are required to bring about better land use decisions.

There are at least two additional rationales for limiting local governmental involvement in major land use decisions. First, most federal environmental programs operate through the states, which are thereby given a strong role in setting environmental standards. If states are setting the standards, some believe, states (rather than local governments) should also be responsible for overseeing compliance with the standards. Second, statewide citizen groups, which have been instrumental in the passage of much land use legislation, find it easier to monitor program operation and performance when responsibilities are centralized at state levels (Bosselman, Feurer, and Siemon 1976).

The Comprehensive-Planning Approach

A number of states have provided local governments a much greater role in achieving state land use objectives. This broader approach, which we term the comprehensive-planning approach, is the subject of this book. Under this approach, states establish comprehensive-planning processes in which they set policy goals and objectives but leave, to varying degrees, the specific details of the content and implementation of plans to the discretion of local governments. By 1993, twelve states, listed in the upper part of table 1.1, had adopted comprehensive-planning programs that either require or strongly encourage local governments to prepare and adopt comprehensive plans. Seven states (listed in the lower part of the table) require some local governments to prepare comprehensive plans as part of substate area planning.

Three basic arguments may be made in favor of delegating responsibility to local governments for meeting state land use objectives. First, in some states local governments have shown a willingness to grapple with land use problems by investing resources in planning and adopting stringent develop-

TABLE 1.1

States with Comprehensive Land Use Management Programs

State	Date[a]	Legislation	Mandated Plans[b]
Statewide			
California	1937	Planning Act	Cities, counties
Colorado	1974	House Bill 1041	Counties (unincorporated areas)
Florida	1972	State Comprehensive Planning Act	State
	1975	Local Government Comprehensive Planning Act	Cities, counties
	1984	State and Regional Planning Act	State, regions
	1985	Local Government Comprehensive Planning and Land Development Regulation Act	Cities, counties
Georgia	1989	Georgia Planning Act	State, regions
Hawaii	1961	State Land Use Law	State (zoning plan)
	1978	Hawaii State Plan	State, cities, counties
Maine	1988	Comprehensive Planning and Land Use Management Act	Regions, cities
Maryland	1992	Economic Growth, Resource Protection, and Planning Act	Counties
New Jersey	1986	State Planning Act	State, 5 planning areas (prepared by state)
Oregon	1975	Land Conservation and Development Act	Cities, counties, Portland area

ment standards. Thus, they are prepared and able to work as partners with state governments in solving important land use problems.

A second argument in favor of a stronger role for local governments is that comprehensive-planning programs, with their emphasis on collaborative planning, recognize the interrelated character of land use decision making. Writing to this point, planning educator Judith Innes notes that "[comprehensive-planning programs] reflect public recognition that many functions of government, from water quality control to transportation, play out and interact on the land. They establish the principle that *both* state and local governments and many public agencies share an interest in *all* uses of land across the state" (Innes 1993, 20; emphasis in original).

A third argument is that comprehensive-planning programs may provide a remedy to a number of potential defects found in the single-purpose

State	Date[a]	Legislation	Mandated Plans[b]
Statewide, continued			
Rhode Island	1988	Comprehensive Planning and Land Use Regulation Act	State, cities, counties
Vermont	1970	Environmental Control Act	State
	1988	Growth Management Act	State, regions
Washington	1990	Growth Management Act	Cities, counties (in fast-growing areas)
Substate Areas			
California	1969	Tahoe Regional Planning Compact	Region
	1972	Coastal Zone Conservation Act	State
	1976	Coastal Act	Cities, counties
Florida	1972	Environmental Land and Water Management Act	None
Maryland	1984	Chesapeake Bay Critical Area Law	Cities, counties
Massachusetts	1974	Martha's Vineyard Commission Act	Region
	1989	Cape Cod Commission Act	Region
New Jersey	1979	State Pinelands Protection Act	Region
New York	1971	Adirondack Park Agency Act	Region
North Carolina	1974	Coastal Area Management Act	Cities, counties (20 coastal counties)

Source: Data from Bollens 1993, DeGrove 1992, Gale 1992, Platt 1991, Salkin 1993.

[a] Year of initial enactment, not including subsequent amendments.

[b] Level of jurisdiction required to develop plans subject to the state mandate.

approach to state land use regulation. For example, environmental lawyer Jon Kusler lists the following shortcomings that may be overcome by the comprehensive approach:

> (1) lack of information pertaining to existing uses, land ownership, local economic conditions, local plans, and local public works policies; (2) substantial transportation and communications barriers in evaluating special permits; (3) political objections to state control based on home rule arguments and desire for local autonomy; and (4) monitoring and enforcement problems due to a lack of field-monitoring devices and inspection staff. (Kusler 1980, 144)

In addition to these problems, planner Frank Popper (1981) notes the frequent exemption of powerful interests (e.g., agriculture and forestry) from coverage by single-purpose state regulatory programs. Such exemptions seem to occur when regulated interests prefer state regulation as a way to escape more restrictive local regulation. These interests can act to prevent state program administrators from developing strong standards or pursuing strong enforcement of single-purpose mandates.

How Important Is Comprehensive Planning?

State mandates for comprehensive planning, and the state land use and growth management systems in which they are embedded, have generated dozens of articles and several books describing individual state efforts or comparing programs across states. But a key question has not yet been answered: do comprehensive-planning mandates have any real impact on local government policy and management of land use? This book answers this question through systematic analysis of the influences that state comprehensive-planning mandates have had on local land use planning and development management. Our approach is framed in part by responding to the limitations of earlier assessments.

Evidence from the first wave of state comprehensive-planning programs suggests that the effects of state mandates on local planning were minor. According to Frank Popper (1981), the programs have had little impact. Jon Kusler, who reviewed the experience of states with programs to protect environmentally sensitive land, concludes: "While comprehensive land planning and regulatory approaches have theoretical attractiveness, they are often beset by political and budgetary problems and hindered by the sheer complexity of issues and analytic needs" (1980, 166). Even an enthusiastic supporter of the comprehensive approach, political scientist John DeGrove (1984), has expressed doubt, noting that the first-wave programs lacked the necessary monitoring and enforcement tools to be effective.

The degree to which performance has improved under the second wave of state planning mandates beginning in the mid-1980s is largely unknown. Most studies of the newer state programs have examined procedural outcomes (e.g., compliance with state prescriptions) based on case studies of individual states. Little research has been done to evaluate the impact on development patterns or the accomplishment of other objectives. In a review of the literature on growth management, planning educator Scott Bollens (1993) concludes that it is difficult to discern broader lessons from the case studies of the newer comprehensive-planning programs because of the use of individual state case analyses and lack of attention to theory. What is needed, he argues, is evidence that state mandates have enhanced local ability to manage growth. This conclusion is also reached by planner Frank Popper (1981), land use lawyer Daniel Mandelker (1989), and economist Gerrit Knaap (1992).

Developing an understanding of the extent and means with which comprehensive-planning mandates influence land use policies and development management by local governments requires more systematic analysis than has been undertaken to date. In this book, we provide this understanding by answering a set of questions revolving around what we identify as the two linchpins of state comprehensive-planning programs. The first is the set of tools the states have available to enlist local governmental cooperation in managing development: Are they sufficient for keeping local governments on track in addressing state policy objectives in land use plans? Do they provide adequate penalties or incentives to foster a high degree of compliance from local governments? The second linchpin is the local comprehensive plan itself: Do plans promulgated in compliance with state mandates substantially affect local management of development? Or, like the "701" plans of an earlier era, are they merely pieces of paper prepared to satisfy state bureaucrats and soon forgotten in the press of day-to-day development management decision making?

In answering these questions, we address the paths through which state requirements for comprehensive planning influence local land use and development management practices. We begin with the ways in which state planning mandates establish the ground rules for local planning and set expectations for relevant state agencies and affected local governments. We then turn to local governments and ask how state mandates affect their willingness to develop plans. Also of interest is the quality of local plans developed in response to state planning mandates. Finally, we consider the actions taken by local governments to manage development. This draws attention to the relation at the local level between comprehensive plans and development management policies.

Our primary interest in the book is establishing the extent and nature of the influence of state comprehensive-planning mandates on local land use plans and development management practices. In studying these, however, it is important to recognize that local development management practices are potentially affected by more than the processes established by state planning mandates. In particular, the single-purpose mandates that states develop to address specific issues are an additional potential influence. The fact that many states have adopted a variety of single-purpose mandates, and fewer have adopted comprehensive-planning programs, leads to a questioning of the necessity of state planning mandates. We address that question by considering what is gained by adding a layer of state comprehensive planning that is not accomplished by the single-purpose mandates. If the planning mandates do not provide adequate tools for implementation, do not lead to better quality plans, or do not enhance local development management actions, then comprehensive state planning programs are likely to add little to the single-purpose mandates whose shortcomings they are supposed to overcome.

In the remainder of this chapter, we provide the foundation for our analyses of comprehensive-planning mandates. This consists of thinking about the two linchpins of state comprehensive-planning programs—the tools that states employ in influencing local planning and the comprehensive local plan itself. We follow that discussion with a presentation of our theory about the paths through which state planning mandates influence local land use plans and development management. We conclude with a discussion of the design of the research upon which this book is based.

Policy Designs for Comprehensive-Planning Mandates

State comprehensive-planning programs differ markedly in two key respects. One is the degree to which states prescribe how local governments should plan for and manage land use. This consists in differences in requirements concerning the consistency of local plans with state goals and policies and differences in specification of the content of local plans. A second difference among state planning mandates is the degree to which states employ various persuasive measures to secure local compliance with state requirements. The following section examines these two aspects of state planning mandates, which together constitute one linchpin in our study of planning mandates.

What Do the States Require?

The key requirement of state comprehensive-planning programs is that local governments prepare plans. However, state planning mandates differ in the specific requirements for the content of local plans. Key distinctions can be made among three types of consistency requirements. *Vertical consistency* requires that local plans be consistent with state goals and policy. This reflects the primary justification for many of the initial state planning programs and is found in most state mandates for local planning. *Horizontal consistency* requires that local plans be coordinated with those of neighboring local governments. It is also present in most state mandates, particularly in the more recently enacted programs. *Local internal consistency* requires that development management activities of local governments be consistent with their comprehensive plans. This entails requirements that local development regulations (e.g., the zoning ordinance) be consistent with the plan or that capital infrastructure be adequate to support whatever private development is permitted by local regulations. The latter is often called a *concurrency requirement*. Together, these consistency requirements define what it is about local planning that is prescribed by a state planning mandate.

Ensuring one or more forms of consistency is a primary justification for state involvement in local planning. The requirements for consistency with state goals and policies (vertical consistency) and with neighboring local governments (horizontal consistency) counter the inclination of local governments to promote purely parochial interests. These two consistency requirements call attention to the interests of neighboring governments and residents of the state as a whole. The internal consistency requirement addresses a historical weakness in much local planning that stems from the lack of connection between a community's plan and its regulations and capital improvements.

The states with more extensive planning requirements include Florida, Vermont, Maine, Rhode Island, and Oregon. Their mandates contain all, or in the case of Oregon all but one, of the consistency requirements discussed above. States making moderate requirements for the local plan include Maryland, New Jersey, Hawaii, North Carolina, and Washington. Each of these states is missing one or more of the three consistency elements and generally have weaker consistency provisions. Washington does not insist on local consistency with state policy objectives. In fact, it requires just the opposite: state agencies must conform their actions to local plans. Maryland and North Carolina do not require coordination among neighboring governments (horizontal consistency). Hawaii, North Carolina, and New Jersey do not require concurrency between planned land use and infrastructure investments. California, Colorado, and Georgia have less extensive requirements. California spells out issues that must be addressed by plans, but it has no horizontal or vertical consistency requirements; Georgia merely encourages consistency. Colorado does not specify requirements for a local plan, and its legislation is generally vague.

How Do the States Persuade Local Governments to Comply?

To varying degrees the states have relied on two sets of tools to convince local governments to prepare plans or otherwise carry out state wishes, either under single-purpose mandates or under comprehensive-planning mandates. Coercion is one. By monitoring local compliance with mandate provisions and imposing sanctions upon localities that do not meet program requirements, states hope to persuade local governments that the costs of not complying are greater than the costs of preparing state-prescribed plans and managing development. Incentives that enhance local capacity to comply are the second set of state tools. By providing financial and technical assistance, states hope to lower compliance costs for localities, thus making it easier for them to follow state requirements.

States with comprehensive-planning mandates vary in the use of these persuasive measures. Florida, Maine, North Carolina, Oregon, and Rhode Island have the strongest set of persuasive features within their planning mandates. These state policies invoke review and approval requirements, make local compliance with state requirements mandatory, impose sanctions for noncompliance, and provide financial and technical assistance for preparation of plans by local governments. The incorporation of persuasive features in planning mandates in Maryland, New Jersey, Vermont, and Washington is less extensive. In New Jersey and Vermont, review of local plans is delegated to regional agencies, compliance by local governments with some provisions is voluntary, and sanctions for local governmental failure to comply with state requirements are more moderate. In Maryland and Washington, the states provide both financial and technical assistance for planning, but the extent of state oversight and ability to impose sanctions on local governments that do not comply are more limited. Persuasion by state agencies is weakest in California, Colorado, Georgia, and Hawaii, where there is little oversight and no sanctions are imposed and, except for Colorado, no financial support is provided to local governments to prepare required plans.

Table 1.2 shows our placement of state comprehensive-planning mandates with respect to the extent of prescriptive and persuasive features contained within each mandate. The table shows that the California, Colorado, and Georgia planning mandates are weak on both dimensions. Hawaii's state planning program is moderately prescriptive but weak in persuasion. Five states—Maryland, New Jersey, North Carolina, Vermont, and Washington—are at least moderate on both dimensions, and one is strong on one dimension. Four states—Florida, Maine, Oregon, and Rhode Island—rank high in the degree of both prescription and persuasion they apply.

It is reasonable to expect that this variation in prescriptive and persuasive elements is matched by similar variation in the quality of local government planning and development management. Given the alleged parochialism of

TABLE 1.2

Key Dimensions of State Mandates

Degree of Persuasion	Degree of Prescription		
	Low	Moderate	High
Low	California, Colorado, Georgia	Hawaii	
Moderate		Maryland, New Jersey, North Carolina, Washington	Vermont
High			Florida, Maine, Oregon, Rhode Island

local governments and their lack of interest in planning, little change from the status quo seems likely unless there are strong state planning requirements. This entails telling local governments what issues to address when planning and insisting on (or otherwise strongly motivating) compliance by local governments with those requirements. We expect comprehensive-planning efforts in states where there are strong state provisions, such as Florida and Oregon, to be much more effective in enhancing local government planning than the much weaker programs in states such as California and Georgia. Other states are expected to fall somewhere between those two extremes. Part of our analysis addresses how differences in the design and implementation of state comprehensive-planning mandates affect the quality and character of local plans and development management actions.

Are Comprehensive Plans Really Necessary?

Perhaps the most fundamental issue this book addresses is the value of local plans. After all, state comprehensive-planning mandates seek to enhance the character and quality of local plans. If local plans are neglected or found to be useless as guides to decisions by local governments about land use and development, then it does not make much sense to set forth state requirements that local governments prepare plans. This draws attention to the second linchpin in our study of state comprehensive-planning mandates: local comprehensive plans. In this section, we summarize relevant literature about plans and their potential for enhancing local decision making about land use and development. We leave it as an empirical question, addressed in later chapters, to assess the extent to which local plans, in fact, influence such decision making.

"Planning" is the label often attached to the broad array of activities that planners undertake. However, most planners not only prepare plans, they also manage land use change. In this regard, the distinction between *plan making* and *development management* is critical (see Kaiser, Godschalk, and Chapin 1995). On the one hand, *plan making* refers to those activities related to the production of a comprehensive plan. The plan is a document that sets forth a community's desired future land use pattern based on factual information about current or projected conditions and analyses of community problems and goals. The plan also makes recommendations for specific government actions. The plan itself, however, does not actually control development. *Development management,* on the other hand, may be viewed as the actual implementation of land use regulations. These include zoning and building codes that impose development standards on the private sector. Development management may be shaped by a plan, but it can (and often does) occur without reference to and in the absence of a plan.

State comprehensive-planning programs are based on the assumption that the data, analysis, rational forethought, and conscious attention to state, regional, and community goals that attend the preparation of a local plan will result in better development management programs. According to planning educators, plans help communities avoid the pitfalls of "nearsighted suboptimization, long-run inconsistency, and the inadvertent creation or aggravation of future land use problems" (Kaiser, Godschalk, and Chapin 1995, 73). They foster better coordination among governmental agencies and programs by providing a common set of facts for use in making decisions and by "obtaining commitments from decision-makers to a coordinated set of actions beyond adoption of general policy guidelines" (ibid., 74). Others (e.g., Haar 1955a; Netter and Mandelker 1981) argue that plans also provide a basis for legal defense when they include a clear statement of the public interest and provide the courts with a meaningful standard for review.

Despite these presumed benefits, the history of planning in the United States casts doubt on the degree to which local comprehensive plans are deemed essential. It is no historical accident that the U.S. Department of Commerce's model Standard Zoning Enabling Act, published in 1922, preceded by six years the department's model Standard City Planning Enabling Act, which was not issued until 1928. Increasing acceptance among local governments of development regulation was viewed as more important than instilling good planning in the formulation of local government policy. That precedent was followed by local governments, many of whom embraced land use regulation prior to and in much greater numbers than land use planning. By the mid-1950s, a survey of local governments found that half of the cities with zoning ordinances had never adopted a comprehensive plan (see Haar 1955b). While many of these communities subsequently prepared plans, their motives were often far different from those suggested by planning theorists. According to political scientists Robert Linowes and Don Allensworth, cities more often than not prepared plans in order to legitimate, rather than to guide, zoning. In their words, "A community zones first, and this gives it the pattern of development it wants . . . and then it brings in planning to 'dress it up' and provide it the Good Housekeeping stamp of approval" (Linowes and Allensworth 1975, 146).

Statewide planning has followed a similar course. Writing from the perspective of the Conservation Foundation, Robert Healy notes: "A comprehensive statewide development plan should eventually be part of every state's land control program. But effective regulation cannot wait until such a plan is prepared" (Healy 1976, 196–97). Furthermore, in some states statewide planning has been greeted by local governments with even less enthusiasm than local planning. Don Benninghover, former director of the California League of Cities, apparently reflected the attitude of many local officials when he asserted that there was "no interest in statewide land use planning in California. None. Not by cities, not by counties, not by the state. . . . We've given up on the grand scheme of doing anything statewide. Instead, we concentrate on legislation on specific problems, such as coastal protection, prime agricultural land, and preserving Lake Tahoe" (quoted in Popper 1988, 296–97).

The "rational paradigm" underlying plan making also has been a target of planning critics. Ernest Alexander (1985), for example, argues that the notion that planners have the capacity to comprehensively plan flies in the face of extensive studies of decision making. These studies include Herbert Simon's (1957) discussion of bounded rationality and Charles Lindblom's (1959) recognition that governments "muddle through" big decisions by making decisions incrementally rather than synoptically. Furthermore, research on public decision making in local government (see Altshuler 1965; Banfield and Meyerson 1955; Catanese 1974) suggests that rational planning processes and the plans emerging from them are out of step with the demands of political decision making and are often simply irrelevant to local policy.

In sum, while the arguments for rational forethought and comprehensive plans seem plausible, there is certainly room for doubt. Local governments have a long history of managing land use without benefit of a plan and seem to have often ignored plans even when they exist. Planning and decision theorists increasingly have questioned the value of the rational paradigm that underlies comprehensive planning. Thus, even if the states are uniformly successful in convincing local governments to prepare plans meeting state specifications, their efforts may still have little effect if the plans themselves are ignored by local governments in their decision making about land use and development.

Theorizing about Mandate Influence

The discussion so far has addressed the two linchpins of state comprehensive-planning programs: the tools that states employ in influencing local planning and the comprehensive local plan itself. However, the understanding of planning mandates that this book seeks to provide requires more than identifying these key components. What is required is delineation of the paths through which state planning mandates potentially influence local land use and development management. Knowing what these are provides a basis for empirical examination of the role and strength of each. What follows, then, is a presentation of our theory about the means by which state mandates influence local planning and the ways in which local plans guide development management. Our theorizing draws from a mix of literature concerning policy design, intergovernmental implementation, regulatory federalism, and planning.

State Mandates and Intergovernmental Implementation

State mandates and their design are central concepts to our theorizing. We conceive of mandates as comprising legislation, administrative rules, and executive orders that require or provide inducements for specified local governmental planning and development management actions (see Advisory Commission on Intergovernmental Relations 1984; Lovell and Tobin 1981). The chief distinction we draw is between comprehensive-planning mandates and single-purpose mandates, reflecting the two basic distinctions drawn earlier in the chapter. The foci of comprehensive-planning mandates are local planning processes and the content, form, and quality of local plans. Single-purpose mandates address development management provisions by directly specifying standards for local private development and the actions local governments must take in fostering compliance with those standards by the private sector.

In thinking about the design of either form of state mandate, we consider two aspects: (1) the set of intentions or goals of the mandate, and (2) the instruments or measures specified in the mandate for accomplishing the intentions. The first aspect consists of the broad objectives of the legislation as might be specified in a preamble or in separate sections. These set the direction and tone of policy. The second set of items acts to structure as well as ease intergovernmental implementation through various inducements, system changes, and commitment- and capacity-building features.

With respect to mandated instruments, there are a variety of items that can potentially be specified. One set is delineation of roles assigned to state and local layers of government, which includes attention to the nature of state review of local plans and the discretion granted to local governments in planning and managing development. Another set of items consists of the tools or measures that local planners are encouraged (or required) to use as part of plan making and development management. This may include encouragement to use innovative planning techniques or particular types of standards when assessing development impacts. A third category comprises the features aimed at building the commitment of local governments to state goals and the capacity of local governments to carry out the policy. We address the commitment- and capacity-building features in more detail below.

State policies also make provisions for and set expectations about the actions of state agencies in carrying out the policies. However, the translation of policy by state agencies into day-to-day actions can be distorted. For example, state agencies may interpret legislative language as setting forth strict requirements when the intent was to be more flexible, or regional offices of state agencies may differ in the degree to which they monitor or enforce state requirements. Disjunctions like these that occur during implementation lead to inconsistencies between state policy on paper and in practice.

There are two aspects to the role of state agencies. One is the effort that relevant agencies put into implementing a given policy. We think of implementation effort as a discount factor applied to state policy intentions. Strong agency implementation effort comprised of many resources devoted to the program and extensive activities entails little discounting of state goals. Weak agency implementation effort in the form of limited attention to the mandate would entail substantial discounting of the mandate intentions.

The second element of the role of state agencies is the character of state agency dealings with local governments. We refer to this as implementation style, which can vary among agencies and states independent of the extent of implementation effort. Stated differently, mandate provisions can in principle be implemented with a range of approaches. Following research on regulatory enforcement (e.g., Kagan 1994; Scholz 1994) and bureaucratic controls (e.g., Gormley 1989; Gruber 1987), we conceptualize the implementation style of state agencies in dealing with local governments as a continuum running from an informal, flexible approach to a formal, legalistic approach. A formal approach is signaled when state policies direct agencies to undertake serious review of local plans and provide authority to impose sanctions for failure to adhere to state requirements. Similarly, a more flexible approach is signaled when a mandate asks state agencies to provide funds, training, or technical assistance to local governments.

We also consider the mix of features aimed at building the commitment and the capacity of local governments to meet state goals to be potentially important in this overall equation. Commitment-building features can range from noncoercive means (e.g., requiring public awareness programs) to coercive means (e.g., sanctions for failure to comply with mandate provisions). Capacity-building features include state-provided technical assistance, training, and funding for local governments.

Local governmental plans and development management measures form the key remaining concepts in our theorizing about mandate influence. As noted earlier, one of the central goals for this book is an understanding of how state mandates affect the character of local planning and development management policies. We distinguish plans and development management ordinances on paper from what is actually undertaken in day-to-day practice in managing development. The on-paper aspects of planning consist of the facts and analysis, goals, and policy recommendations found in local comprehensive plans. The on-paper aspects of development management consist of the set of measures adopted by ordinance that local governments employ for managing development. Following various theorizing about environmental regulation (e.g., Hedge, Menzel, and Krause 1989; Scholz 1991; Scholz and Wei 1986), we assume that local governments modify state policy provisions to fit local circumstances. The extent and type of this adaptation are presumed to be influenced by local political and economic factors as well as by the mix of commitment- and capacity-building features within state mandates.

The preceding discussion might suggest that the deck is stacked against state planning mandates becoming important vehicles for enhancing local planning or development management. Indeed, much of the relevant literature suggests a world in which planners and, by extension, state policy makers are largely captive to local circumstances. In keeping with this perspective, we consider how the local context shapes planning opportunities and constrains development management. In particular, we consider the challenges in managing development faced by local officials and the political and economic environment within which local officials make decisions about development.

Yet this book addresses the fundamental proposition that state policies can influence decisions by local governments about land use and development. The theory presented here leads us to believe that the extent of this influence rests on several key factors. One is the state mandate itself and the extent to which it articulates clear goals and provides a framework through the right mix of commitment- and capacity-building provisions for fostering local government adherence to state objectives. A second factor is the effort that state agencies put into carrying out the policy, as indicated by such things as the seriousness with which they undertake technical assistance and review activities. A third factor is the character of state agency dealings with local governments on a day-to-day basis, for which the central issue is the extent to which the agency implementation style is consistent with the intent of the state policy. A final set of factors is the normative commitment of local governments to participate in state programs (i.e., their willingness to develop plans) and the capacity of local agencies to undertake the requisite tasks.

Mandates, Local Planning, and Development Management

State mandates are aimed at affecting decisions made by local governments. The focal point of comprehensive-planning mandates is local plans—the facts, goals, and policy recommendations that constitute a local plan. State requirements concerning plan content directly affect the character of local plans. Through specification of required planning elements (e.g., consistency requirements) and procedures, planning mandates establish a set of expectations for local governmental action. These expectations may not always be fulfilled and may be modified by local governments to better fit local circumstances. Much depends on the particulars of the expectations, whether local governments are being asked to undertake tasks that are appropriate to their needs, and local situational factors.

State planning mandates also affect the commitment of local governments to state goals and the capacity of local governments to carry out planning. We think of commitment as endorsement of state mandate goals by local officials and relevant local government agency heads. We think of capacity as the ability of local governments to accomplish objectives set forth in state mandates. From this perspective, state planning mandates and the local plans they require are not merely ends in themselves. They are also tools to persuade and enable local officials to embrace state policy objectives.

In thinking about this aspect of planning mandates, it is useful to draw a distinction between the commitment to plan and the commitment to particular policy objectives. Planning mandates attempt to influence the former by providing incentives for local governments to develop plans or by applying sanctions when local governments fail to develop required plans. The emphasis is on obtaining procedural compliance by affecting calculations that local officials make about the importance of preparing plans. We refer to this as calculated commitment. The presumption is that the process of developing a plan will lead to a greater understanding of policy problems posed by improper land use or development. This understanding presumably leads to a greater willingness, which we term normative commitment, to address such problems. As a consequence, local officials are presumed to be motivated to address the problems following recommendations made in the plan.

There is also a potentially important political dynamic associated with plan making. Plans can empower citizens to become active in demanding governmental attention to improper land use or development. That can occur in two ways. First, the information provided in a plan serves a frame-setting function that helps both citizens and government decision makers better understand their situation (Alexander 1992; Faludi 1987). Second, when plans actually involve citizens in problem solving, they can reduce conflict and produce consensus about how governments should address land use and development problems. By fostering what planning theorists term communicative rationality rather than (or in addition to) pure technical rationality, plans can result in broad-based support for the recommendations they contain. This, in turn, can result in greater demands on policy makers to commit to and carry forward these recommendations.

The relations between local plans and development management measures gets to the heart of our theorizing about the implementation of development management programs. Much of the plan-making literature argues that plans provide needed information, a consensus on goals, and analyses for formulating effective programs for development management (for a synthesis of the literature, see Kaiser, Godschalk, and Chapin 1995). As such, the plan provides a guide to local policies that presumably shape development management measures.

However, we think the link between plans and development management is much more fragile. When plans address issues that are not high on local political agendas or run counter to the interests of powerful groups within a community, potentially relevant plan recommendations can be ignored. In addition, the timing of the adoption of plans, development management ordinances, and other measures can be problematic. In many communities, development management ordinances predate plans. In others, plans have been written and adopted but not revised or kept up to date.

State comprehensive-planning mandates can strengthen the planning and development management linkage by requiring that development management actions be consistent with local plans. However, consistency is not sufficient if the local plans are of poor quality. It is difficult to guide development management with a poorly defined plan. For this reason, plan quality is also a central element in our theorizing and empirical work.

As a consequence of the variety of considerations raised in the preceding paragraphs, we can expect different degrees of success among state planning mandates with respect to their influence on land use and development actions. Not only might the content of local plans differ from mandate expectations, but so might the timing. As noted in the implementation literature (Mazmanian and Sabatier 1983; Goggin et al. 1990), there are a variety of possible scenarios concerning the timing of implementation, ranging from speedy implementation to delayed or eroded implementation. Local governments may willingly embrace mandate provisions, or they may be more reluctant and simply comply perfunctorily. A local plan could technically meet state requirements but may not be acted upon if the plan was prepared reluctantly in response to state coercion.

From Theorizing to Policy Research

The preceding discussion provides our theory about the paths through which state planning mandates potentially influence local land use and development management. Specification of these paths provides a basis for empirical examination of the role and strength of each. Not surprisingly, there is somewhat of a leap from the explication of our theory about mandate influence to the findings of subsequent chapters. In making this transition, it is useful for us to be clear about the choices we have made in designing the research and about the foci of the study.

An Overview of the Research Design

By comparing the experience of local governments in states (and substate areas) with and without comprehensive-planning mandates, we are able to empirically evaluate the influence of mandates on local plans and the influence of mandates and plans on local development management. Much of the prior research on planning mandates and growth management consists of case studies of a single mandate for a particular state. Measuring mandate influence, however, requires speculation about the counterfactual—what would have happened without a mandate. By comparing experiences in states with and without comprehensive-planning mandates and by including appropriate statistical controls for the comparison, we are able to successfully gauge mandate influence.

We analyze local government experiences with planning and development management in five states. The basic comparison is between states that have comprehensive-planning mandates and those that do not. The states we study that have comprehensive-planning mandates are California and Florida, which mandate comprehensive planning statewide, and North Carolina, which mandates comprehensive planning in twenty coastal counties. Those three states span the range of mandate designs shown earlier in table 1.2. Florida's program features the use of strong prescriptive and persuasive measures; North Carolina's occupies a middle position, employing a moderate number of prescriptive and persuasive measures; and California's mandate is relatively weak, with few prescriptions and little state effort to persuade local governments to comply. The states (or substate areas) selected for our study that lack comprehensive-planning mandates are Texas, North Carolina's twenty mountain counties, and Washington state. (Our study was conducted prior to the implementation in 1990 of the state of Washington's growth management legislation.) These areas were selected because of their similarity in demographic characteristics and land use problems to the three states with planning mandates.

Our assessment of the paths through which state planning mandates potentially influence local land use and development management entails a variety of empirical analyses. The starting point for the empirical assessment is the design of state planning mandates, which provides an understanding of the state requirements for plans and the tools states use to persuade local governments to carry out planning. We evaluate the realities of state planning programs by considering the day-to-day actions of relevant state agencies in dealing with local governments. We consider the extent of effort that state agencies devote to policy implementation and the character of their dealings with local governments.

We also consider the direct and indirect influences that state planning mandates have upon local planning and plan quality. We get at these issues in two ways. First, we use findings from our surveys of local governments in order to characterize the extent to which localities undertake planning, the commitment of local officials to planning, and the capacity of local agencies to plan. Second, where local plans exist, we evaluate the quality of the plans according to benchmarks set forth later in the book. Of particular interest is the extent to which the willingness of localities to plan and the quality of local plans are affected by the presence or absence of state planning mandates.

The relation between local plans and development management gets to the heart of the presumed value of comprehensive plans in guiding development decisions. We employ data gathered from our surveys of local governments to evaluate the relation between plans and development management at the local level. This draws attention to the role of better-quality plans in affecting development management and to the nature of differing plan recommendations.

Natural Hazards as a Topical Focus

Each of the state planning mandates under study requires local governments to develop plans for guiding decisions regarding land use and development. However, the mandates differ somewhat in the range of issues to which local governments are asked to attend. Given the differences in scope and focus of these policies, we found it necessary to identify common elements for study. To provide this, we choose to focus on the natural hazards components of each policy mandate. This provides a focus for the comparison and a tractable set of planning and development issues to study. As explained here, we consider local governmental management of land use and development in hazard-prone areas a viable yardstick for measuring the influence of state mandates on local government planning and development management.

The natural hazards components of the planning mandates under study consist of various planning provisions dealing with land use and development in areas subject to one or more of the following: earthquakes, floods, hurricanes, landslides. These provisions range in specificity from general requirements that local governments specify planning policies that address development in hazard-prone areas to more specific requirements. The latter include requirements, for example in Florida, that localities identify populations at risk from natural hazards and develop plans for addressing those risks. In both Florida and North Carolina, the state planning requirements include attention to evacuation in the aftermath of a catastrophic event. More generally, the state planning provisions relating to local decisions about development in hazard-prone areas look much like the planning provisions for any form of development. Localities are asked as part of planning processes to craft policies for managing development using appropriate tools for the task at hand.

Although it is not the first issue that normally comes to mind when thinking about planning, how natural hazards are addressed as part of local plans raises a number of issues that are illustrative of broader planning issues. The strong state interest in protecting lives and reducing losses from natural disasters provides an impetus for requirements that localities consider planning solutions to development problems in hazard-prone areas. The prevalence of these issues as planning problems is evident from the fact that virtually every local government in the United States has to contend with at least one form of natural hazard. The possibilities for planning solutions has long been advocated by hazards researchers who see land use and development management as keys to mitigating risks posed by natural disasters.

Like debates on land use more generally, debates about controlling development in hazardous areas often focus on resource capacity, environmental protection, and economic development issues. Decisions made by local governments about appropriate uses of land, controls over development, or regulation of construction in hazardous areas can have profound effects on economic vitality, environmental quality, and vulnerability to natural events. Like other aspects of local planning, the stakes in making these decisions are often large, and conflicts over the outcomes are not easily resolved.

Data Collection and Measurement

We leave the details of data collection and measurement to a methodological appendix and provide an overview here. Our understanding and analysis of experiences with comprehensive and single-purpose state mandates are based on several sources of information. Within each state and the North Carolina coastal and mountain regions, we selected a random sample of 30 local governments for evaluation. Four declined to participate, which left a final sample of 176 governments, 88 subject to planning mandates and 88 not subject to such mandates. We administered questionnaires to the sample of local governments and evaluated plan quality for those governments that had prepared comprehensive plans.

Our understanding of the features of state mandates and the efforts made by relevant state agencies was gained from several sources. First, we searched the literature to develop a narrative description of the historical evolution of each mandate. Second, we collected the formal legislation and administrative rules to measure characteristics of the mandates "on paper." Third, we interviewed agency administrators to learn about how the mandates were implemented. Fourth, we used self-administered questionnaires to gather information about resources committed to the mandates and to learn from agency administrators how the mandates were implemented.

In tandem, the quantitative and qualitative data we assembled from state agencies, local governments, and various secondary sources provide the most complete assessment to date of state planning mandates and their implementation. More important, these data also allow us to go beyond simple description to provide a rigorous, credible assessment of planning mandates and their effects on local planning and development management.

I

State Experiments in Managing Land Use

2

California
Coping with Congestion

Responding to decades of explosive growth, California has used comprehensive-planning and single-purpose mandates to force local governments to deal with critical problems of statewide concern. With a strong tradition of home rule and enormous diversity in local conditions (Stone and Seymour 1993), however, state legislators do not insist that local governments adhere to a comprehensive set of state policy goals. Instead, the California planning mandate requires local governments to prepare plans for specific planning elements, such as land use and housing. The list of elements has been expanded over time as problems the state believes local governments should address have gained wide recognition. State-required local comprehensive plans (termed general plans in California) are used to coordinate the array of state directives and adapt them to local conditions. In this chapter, we describe the evolution and defining characteristics of the California approach to managing growth.

Setting the Stage

California and urban growth are synonymous. With just 1.5 million residents in 1900, the state more than quadrupled in population by 1940, and it literally exploded after World War II, reaching more than 30 million by 1990. In 1996, eight of every ten Californians live in urban areas located within thirty miles of the Pacific. This congestion has created a recipe for disaster. California has a virtual stew of natural hazards—seismic faults, unstable slopes, eroding shore lands, volcanic zones, fire-prone brushland, and flash-flood areas—that when mixed with dense development has produced catastrophic results.

Recurring disasters have been a fact of life, making California the leading recipient of federal public disaster assistance in the 1980s. With billions in property damages in the 1989 Loma Prieta (San Francisco–area) and 1994 Northridge (Los Angeles–area) earthquakes, viewed by millions on national television, and massive wildfire losses in the 1991 Oakland Hills and 1993 southern California fires, the state's vulnerability continues to attract attention from both state and federal lawmakers.

State-Mandated Comprehensive Planning

California was the first state to make local governments plan. In 1927 all cities and counties were authorized, and in 1937 required, to adopt comprehensive plans. As state legislators struggled to cope with postwar growth, they began to tell local governments what those plans had to address. The legislature added requirements for land use and circulation elements in 1955, a housing element in 1967, conservation and open-space elements in 1970, and seismic safety and two other elements in 1971. The addition of required elements one by one typifies California's ad hoc response to problems arising from rapid growth. The consequence has been a similar ad hoc approach to comprehensive planning, with each plan element functioning as a separate document rather than as part of a well-integrated policy for future development.

Implementing the Planning Mandate

The state planning mandate requires 461 cities and 58 counties to each adopt "a comprehensive, long-term general plan for the physical development of the city or county and any land outside its boundaries which in the planning agency's judgment bears relation to its planning" (California Government Code § 65300). The Office of Planning and Research (OPR) in the governor's office is the main implementing agency, and it offers technical assistance to help local governments meet the requirements of the mandate.

Initially, the governor's office provided little guidance on how to comply with the mandate to plan. In the 1970s, however, litigation over the adequacy of particular general plans increased, which suggested that more direction was needed to help planners comply with the law. After several years of work, new, greatly expanded guidelines were distributed to local governments in 1980 and were updated again in 1983 and 1987. The guidelines are advisory only and do not have the force of law. Nevertheless, they contain numerous specifications for the content of plans and the process of preparing them. For example, the state guidelines recommend that plans be long term, comprehensive, and internally consistent. Amendments are to occur no more than four times per year. Plan documents are to include a statement of development policies and text explaining the plan's objectives, principles, standards, and proposals for government action.

California planning legislation does not specify a deadline for preparation of plan elements, nor does it require periodic updates to keep plans current (advisory guidelines, however, suggest major updates every four or five years). Also, the state has no sanctions it can apply if local governments fail to plan. With the exception of the housing and safety elements, it does not even review local plans. Instead, California has used the judicial system to enforce its planning legislation.

Key Role of Citizens and the Judiciary in Implementation

The requirements and meaning of the underlying planning statute have been the subject of much citizen-initiated litigation. Many of the strengths of the act emerged from these court decisions, whereas in other states with planning mandates, administrative interpretation has played a more important role. The California courts have held the general plan to be "a constitution for all future development," so that local zoning laws must conform to the adopted general plan (see *Friends of B Street v City of Hayward* and *Neighborhood Action Group v County of Calaveras*). Courts have the authority to review general plans for substantial compliance with provisions of the planning act. If a plan is found wanting, the courts have issued injunctions against new development as an appropriate remedy and spur to force local governments to adopt an adequate plan. Additionally, the planning statute has been held by the courts to be the source of standards that plan elements must meet to be deemed adequate, but the judiciary has refused to make the guidelines prepared by the governor's office anything more than advisory.

In addition to lawsuits to force local compliance with the provisions of state planning statutes, California citizens have another, rather unique, tool to affect local planning decisions. Local voters are empowered by the California Constitution to use initiatives and referendums to enact or repeal land use planning provisions and zoning and other land use regulations (Caves 1992; Stone and Seymour 1993). In framing initiatives and referendums, however, citizens have to comply with the substantive provisions of state planning statutes. Thus, this is another tool to strengthen compliance with, rather than circumvent, state planning authority.

Approach to Natural Hazards

By law, one element of the comprehensive plan must address safety. Safety and seismic safety elements were first required in 1971, largely in response to losses suffered in the San Fernando earthquake, which killed sixty-four persons and caused $500 million in property damages. Six years later, the California Seismic Safety Commission surveyed local governments to see what had been accomplished by requiring attention to earthquake hazards in plan making. According to the commission, localities were paying more attention to seismic hazards than they had in the 1960s, but the separate consideration of earthquake and other natural hazards in plans seemed to be wasteful of staff resources and to limit opportunities to find ways of mitigating risks that are common to a number of different natural hazards. The commission also felt that localities were paying too much attention to gathering information about seismic risk and not enough to formulating policies to reduce risk. The state legislature acted on the commission findings seven years later by mandating that local governments combine the seismic safety and safety elements of plans and include hazard mitigation as a focal point of planning for safety.

The safety element is supposed to protect communities from unreasonable risks due to seismic activity, landslides, subsidence, flooding, and fires by providing geologic hazard maps, evacuation plans, and suggestions for mitigation of hazards. The California Division of Mines and Geology reviews and comments on locally prepared safety elements, but it does not have the power to formally approve or reject whatever local governments put forward. The law requires city and county legislative bodies to consider, but not necessarily to follow, the recommendations of the division prior to formally adopting a plan. Thus, although a copy of the local safety element is filed with the state, California state officials have no formal power to amend or reject the local planning effort.

Evaluation of the Planning Legislation

The California planning mandate has not been the subject of previous scholarly research, although several state-sponsored evaluations have been conducted and several studies have looked at implementation of specific plan elements (Olshansky 1993). The Special Subcommittee on Community Development of the California Assembly evaluated the planning act in 1976 and 1977. The 1976 study reported that local administrators found mandated plans to be ineffective in guiding growth. The subcommittee also found that plan elements were inconsistent and unrelated to one another and that local administrators felt the mandated elements created unnecessary work. To resolve these problems, it recommended that the planning act be revised to combine local planning, budgeting, and community development processes and to provide incentives for especially effective local planning.

The 1977 report found no relation between the mandated functional plans of special districts and the local general plans prepared by cities and counties. It called for a statutory requirement of consistency among all state-mandated planning. The 1976 and 1977 studies, however, did not result in subsequent legislation.

The safety element also has been evaluated on several occasions. A study by the Seismic Safety Element Review Committee in 1985 found that the safety element raised the awareness of planners, decision makers, and the general public; however, the committee also found it did not serve as an adequate guide for local action to mitigate seismic hazards. Studies documenting difficulties implementing the hazards elements of plans are rare, and their findings are inconsistent. In a study of thirteen general plans, University of California at Santa Barbara political scientists Alan Wyner and Dean Mann concluded:

> Resource allocation for implementation of seismic safety policy has been virtually nonexistent. Most jurisdictions have chosen not to allocate monetary or non-monetary resources in a manner that would permit fulfillment of the adopted goals; most jurisdictions have made only slight movement toward goal accomplishment. Whatever level of risk was accepted in the adoption of the SSE [Seismic Safety Element], very little has been done to make it a reality through policy implementation. (Wyner and Mann 1983, 321–22)

A two-part study by University of California city and regional planners (Cook 1990; Cornwall 1990), based on a survey of sixteen cities and counties and a review of environmental impact reports, came to similar conclusions. But planners Laurence Mintier and Peter Stromberg studied seven cities for the Division of Mines and Geology and reported that policies regarding existing hazardous buildings had been universally adopted, and most governments had adopted policies to reduce damage to critical facilities (Mintier and Stromberg 1983).

Single-Purpose Mandates

In addition to requiring the safety element in the general plan, the State of California has used a number of single-purpose mandates to force local governments to deal with various issues related to natural hazards. Some of these, such as the state building law, have only a tangential connection to the general-plan safety element. Others, such as the coastal zone management program and environmental impact assessment requirements, are closely linked to local plans. Here we look at the nature of these mandates and the ways in which they may reinforce the commitment of local governments to address natural hazards.

CEQA: A State Mandate to Consider Natural Hazards in Granting Development Permits

Legislators enacted the 1970 California Environmental Quality Act (CEQA) to inform decision makers and the public of potential adverse environmental effects from government actions and, where feasible, to avoid or mitigate environmental damage. The legislation faced little opposition, in part because local governments and development interests thought it applied only to projects directly undertaken by state agencies. Within a year of the CEQA's passage, however, the California Supreme Court held in *Friends of Mammoth v Board of Supervisors* that the act requires environmental analyses of private as well as public projects.

Following a preliminary review of a proposed project to see if it is exempt from provisions of the act, the CEQA requires cities and counties to conduct an "Initial Study" to identify potentially significant environmental effects. If no effect is found, a "Negative Declaration" is issued and the project can move forward. If the possibility of environmental harm exists, an "Environmental Impact Report" (EIR) is required. Because of the time and cost required for an EIR, many developers choose to mitigate potential adverse effects, in which case the permitting government issues a "Mitigated Negative Declaration." When the initial study reveals mitigation is not feasible or the developer chooses not to mitigate adverse effects, a full-scale environmental impact report must be prepared. If the report subsequently reveals significant adverse environmental effects will result from a project, then either these effects must be mitigated before development permits can be issued or the governing body must make a finding of "Overriding Considerations" for project approval without mitigation. A survey in 1991 found that most projects requiring an EIR are approved for development, and in a majority of these cases, approval comes not from mitigation but from a local government finding of overriding considerations (Olshansky 1993).

Initial studies and environmental impact reports both must consider vulnerability to natural hazards and the effects a proposed project will have on the exposure of other property to hazards. But consideration of hazards is often perfunctory (Cornwall 1990), and no sanctions or enforcement mechanisms are provided to penalize developers or local governments that do not comply with the law. Instead, litigation is the only tool for enforcement. However, following revelations that developers failed to install half or more of the measures they had proposed to obtain mitigated negative declarations, the legislature amended the CEQA in 1988 to require monitoring of compliance (California Resources Code § 21081.6).

The California Environmental Quality Act has been criticized for the costs and uncertainties it adds to the development process. In 1979, in response to one such attack, the legislature amended the objectives of the law in order to foster greater balance between environmental and economic ends. With the revised goals, the purpose of the CEQA is to foster "the long-term protection of the environment, *consistent with the provision of a decent home and a suitable living environment for every Californian*" (italics added).

In the early 1990s, the program came under attack again because of its alleged costs to the private sector. The Governor's Council on California Competitiveness recommended in 1992 that local comprehensive plans, rather than the CEQA, serve as the primary vehicle for environmental review and assessment, but the legislature did not accept this recommendation. In fact, a 1991 survey of 355 city and county planners in California by Robert Olshansky (1993) reveals that most planners believed the CEQA reinforces, rather than duplicates, information provided by the general plan. The reason for this stems, in part, from the tendency of general plans to become outdated. Olshansky found 20 percent of the cities and counties he surveyed had not updated their plans in over a decade. As a consequence, the CEQA provides more-current information upon which to base decisions.

Seismic Safety Mandates

In addition to seismic safety provisions of its planning legislation and the seismic code provisions of the Uniform Building Code (which all cities and counties are required to adopt), California has three main statutes aimed specifically at seismic safety in the built environment. The Alquist-Priolo Special Studies Zones Act is designed to prevent development in active fault zones. The Unreinforced Masonry Law seeks to identify and then strengthen highly vulnerable unreinforced masonry buildings. The Seismic Hazards Mapping Act establishes a program aimed at fostering use of information about seismic hazards in local planning.

Like the required seismic safety element of the general plan, the 1971 Alquist-Priolo Special Studies Zones Act was enacted in response to the San Fernando earthquake. The act requires cities and counties to restrict future development on active faults and directs the state geologist to identify fault zones that present a potential hazard. In addition, local governments are required to inform the public of the presence of fault zones through their general plans or other maps. The zones are limited to a maximum width of a quarter of a mile. Applications for development in the zones must include a geologic report, and city or county approval is necessary if the development is intended for human occupancy. Approvals must be consistent with state Mining and Geology Board policies and criteria. The act was amended in 1975 to require disclosure of seismic hazards to people purchasing property located in seismic fault zones.

In 1989, the Division of Mines and Geology hired a consultant to evaluate the effectiveness of this act (Reitherman 1992). All affected jurisdictions were surveyed, along with consulting geologists, state agencies, and real estate firms. The consultant found the program to be generally effective in its limited purpose of minimizing development along fault zones. Others (Palm 1981), however, have judged the real estate disclosure requirements to be ineffective.

The 1990 Seismic Hazards Mapping Act expanded the Alquist-Priolo mapping program to other hazards (Reitherman 1992). This legislation launched an ambitious effort to map, at state expense, areas subject to strong ground shaking, liquefaction, landslides, and other ground failures. Local governments are responsible for making the resulting seismic information available to the public. The act incorporates the disclosure and special study provisions of the previous Alquist-Priolo seismic zone act.

The Unreinforced Masonry, or URM, Law was enacted in 1986 (California Government Code § 8875 et seq.). It requires identification and mitigation of hazards in buildings with any unreinforced masonry walls. Local governments in the most earthquake-prone regions of the state (Seismic Zone Four) are required to inventory all unreinforced masonry buildings that are potentially hazardous, develop and implement local hazard mitigation programs, and submit information on the potentially hazardous buildings and mitigation programs to the state Seismic Safety Commission (SSC). Seismic Zone Four includes the major metropolitan areas of Los Angeles and San Francisco, with a total population of nearly 23 million. Information submitted to the SSC is used to track progress toward safety objectives and to identify needed state assistance. In the case of the URM law, however, the SSC reported in 1991 that lack of funding, potential loss of low-income housing, tenant dislocation, and potential loss of historic buildings had all slowed implementation (Comerio 1992).

Flood Hazard Mandates

The 1965 Cobey-Alquist Floodplain Management Act encourages local governments to adopt and enforce land use regulations for designated floodways and provides state financial assistance for flood control (California Water Code § 8401 et seq.). In 1972, the state amended the legislation to add sanctions for noncompliance: state aid for acquiring property for flood control projects is withheld unless floodplain regulations for the designated floodway have been adopted, and flood control districts are authorized to adopt and enforce the needed regulations if cities or counties fail to act.

Coastal Hazard Mandates

The California Coastal Zone Conservation Act, enacted in 1972 when the voters approved Proposition 20, created a statewide commission and six regional commissions to develop a long-range plan for the California coast and to regulate development activity in an area extending one thousand feet inland from the ocean. The California Coastal Plan, submitted to the legislature in 1975, proposed a framework for managing coastal resources based on state goals and policies that would be effectuated primarily through local general plans and development regulations. A variety of coastal problems (energy, transportation, public access, recreation, protection of coastal waters and lands, and coastal appearance and design) were dealt with in the plan, but none of the 162 policy recommendations specifically addressed natural hazards.

The coastal plan was adopted in 1976 through the Coastal Act, which established California's coastal zone management program. The act requires local governments to prepare coastal programs consistent with state goals and policies. After the local plans and implementing regulations are certified as in compliance with state standards, the authority to grant permits is transferred from the state to the locality. The state coastal commission reviews certified local coastal programs at least once every five years. Because the review does not entail recertification, however, it may have little effect.

From its inception, the California coastal program has been characterized by strained state-local relations. State coastal advocates and planners blamed local governments for many of the coast's problems as a strategy to win support for state intervention. That won them few friends among local planners. In addition, the state staff has studiously avoided making decisions on the basis of local public opinion. In the words of state staff director Michael Fischer, "the California Coastal Commission planners would not, could not, and assertively did not recognize or respect local political realities" (1985, 316). As a result of these and other factors, local governments were slow to prepare local coastal programs. A decade after adoption of the Coastal Plan, 20 percent of 123 coastal planning areas did not have state-certified land use plans, and 58 percent lacked state-certified implementation programs required for local permitting under the act. Thus, through the mid-1980s, most permit decisions were made at the state rather than the local level.

Concluding Note

Although the rate of growth slowed after 1990, growth management continues to be an important issue in California, in part because policy makers are beginning to realize that the ad hoc state-mandated planning system can not cope adequately with a variety of urban growth issues. Throughout the first years of the 1990s, efforts were under way to overhaul the state planning system, but by the middle of the decade, little had been accomplished.

In 1990, Pete Wilson was elected governor in a campaign that placed great emphasis on growth management issues. Wilson formed an Interagency Council on Growth Management to develop recommendations for a statewide plan. Public hearings held throughout the state revealed that traffic congestion, lack of affordable housing, water shortages, loss of resource land, and the cost of growth were the issues of greatest concern. The council reached agreement on the need for a comprehensive state plan to guide local government management of development and on the importance of strengthening regional cooperation through existing organizations such as councils of government. Legislation to authorize preparation of a state plan, however, has not been considered.

A Growth Management Consensus Project sponsored by the state assembly and senate offices of research held a series of meetings in 1990 attended by an array of interest groups with a stake in urban growth. Some of the project's findings, such as the need for consistent state policies, echoed those of the interagency council. However, consensus could not be reached on many significant points: Who should decide whether local policies are consistent with state policies and regional strategies? How can a regional authority be established without creating another level of government? Should state oversight extend to the review of specific development proposals or should it be limited to state review and approval of local general plans?

Although California launched state-mandated local comprehensive planning in the United States, it has failed to keep pace with innovations in mandate design forged by other states, such as preparation of a state comprehensive plan and requirements for consistency with state goals in local plan making. With a strong tradition of home rule, which the state legislature has been reluctant to intrude upon, it also never has been able to insert strong state oversight provisions into the planning mandate. As a consequence, local governments have a considerable degree of autonomy in their plan making.

3

North Carolina
Mandated Planning to Protect the Coast

In the face of booming oceanfront development beginning in the 1950s, North Carolina passed an array of single-purpose laws to deal with specific problems—encroachment on frontal dunes, loss of wetlands, and pollution of oyster beds. In the early 1970s, spurred by the federal coastal program, the state began to explore a more coordinated approach to land management. The outcome was the 1974 Coastal Area Management Act, an innovative law that mandates state regulation and local planning to protect coastal resources. With this legislation, state policy makers folded an array of single-purpose environmental regulations into one comprehensive state regulatory program. It called on local governments in coastal areas to plan for the balanced, wise use of land and to join the state in regulating particularly sensitive areas such as hurricane-prone shore lands. The resulting state-local partnership has been hailed as a national model for effective coastal zone management (see DeGrove 1984).

Setting the Stage

The 1970s were momentous times for North Carolina. After years of steady net out-migration from this predominantly rural state, between 1970 and 1980 net in-migration accounted for nearly half of the state's population growth. Many of the new Tarheels settled in the Piedmont Crescent—the home of the state's textile, furniture, and tobacco industries—and the Research Triangle Park, with its array of computer, communications, and pharmaceutical firms. But surprising to many, growth accelerated in previously slow-growing rural places, too, particularly in the scenically attractive, environmentally sensitive Tidewater and mountain regions. In the 1970s, for example, growth in Dare County along the Outer Banks exploded to almost 10 percent per year (and over 20 percent per year in Cape Hatteras Township). In the mountains, retirement communities swelled populations in places such as Henderson County near Asheville, which grew at over 3 percent per year. This is double the statewide rate of increase in the number of older persons.

Environmental degradation in the coastal region attracted the attention of policy makers first. North Carolina marine resources include more than 3,375 miles of tidal shoreline and 4,650 square miles of estuarine waters. Surpassed in size only by those of Alaska and Louisiana, the state's estuaries support a variety of habitats and biological communities—salt marshes, oyster reefs, sand and mud bottoms, and intertidal mud flats—and economically important commercial and sports fisheries. By the 1970s, these resources were reeling from the impacts of population growth. Particularly disturbing to people throughout North Carolina, by 1972 fully one-quarter of the state's 2 million acres of shellfish waters were closed to harvesting due to pollution (North Carolina Marine Science Council 1972). People as well as animals were at risk. Hurricane Hazel leveled barrier island communities in 1954, but people quickly rebuilt at even higher densities. By the end of the 1970s, fully a third of the barrier islands in North Carolina had been developed in a string of sprawling residential and resort communities.

The mountain region was also hard hit by newfound prosperity. Visual blight came to a boil when developers leveled the top of local landmark Little Sugar Mountain and replaced it with a new peak—a high-rise condominium. That led to a state Ridge Law, banning future mountain topping, but not a comprehensive effort to deal with other environmental problems. As Appalachian State University geographers Ole Gade and Dan Stillwell complained,

> We are in a region faced with an environment peculiarly sensitive to land speculation and development which is goaded by private and corporate pecuniary self interest operating largely in locally permissive political arenas. Though the evidence of environmental neglect, if not actual destruction, is rapidly accumulating, North Carolinians have responded in a hesitating and spotty fashion. Where region-wide action is demanded only highly localized solutions are proffered. (Gade and Stillwell 1986, 200)

In the early 1970s, like their coastal counterparts, only one in five mountain local governments had a land use plan or any land use regulation (see Burby 1977; Haskell 1976). But throughout the period studied for this book, the mountain region failed to receive the attention state policy makers gave to the Tidewater, North Carolina's other threatened environment.

Managing Land Use in the Tidewater

North Carolina has mandated comprehensive planning only in the coastal zone. This mandate came after fifteen years of experimentation with a variety of single-purpose environmental protection laws. The first was the 1959 State Lands Act (implemented in 1965), which placed limits on the conveyance of state-owned wetlands and established a general policy that wetlands should be preserved. Responding to explosive development along the Outer Banks, in the 1965 Sand Dune Protection Act the state authorized (but did not require) local governments to prohibit the alteration of dunes oceanward of a shore protection line. When only two local governments used this new authority, in 1969 the General Assembly required local regulation of frontal sand dunes. Reflecting strong national interest in the environment and coastal areas that year, the state also enacted a dredge-and-fill law, appropriated funds to acquire estuarine shoreline, and asked the state commissioner of commercial and sport fisheries to develop a comprehensive management plan for the coastal zone by 1973.

In 1970, Governor Robert Scott first considered a proposal to establish a state coastal zone management program, but he decided to pursue other environmental regulations, instead. The General Assembly passed a Coastal Wetlands Act in 1971, which authorized rule-making procedures to regulate land development in coastal marshes subject to tidal influence. That same year, the commissioner of commercial and sport fisheries established a Comprehensive Estuarine Blue Ribbon Committee to respond to various drafts of a state coastal management bill then being developed. When Jim Holshouser, the state's first Republican governor in the twentieth century, took office in 1973, he was greeted with the results of the Blue Ribbon Committee's deliberations—a proposal for a comprehensive law to centralize management of coastal resources.

An advocate of responsible land use management, the governor backed the proposal, but interim public hearings revealed intense local opposition (Heath 1974). Local hostility came from two sources. City and county officials resented state interference in what they viewed as a wholly local realm of decision making, while economic development interests feared the proposal would stifle economic growth. A representative of the banking industry commented at the time, "We're spending tens of millions of dollars on technical schools in North Carolina to teach people to participate in modern society. If we were to be so foolish as to adopt this no-growth legislation, it would be the cruelest sort of action. These people would be all ready to get out of school with no place to go" (cited in Healy 1976, 169). Rather than risk defeat in the General Assembly, Governor Holshouser bowed to local concerns and delayed the legislation.

In 1974, he offered a substantially different bill. The new version increased the involvement of local governments in the planning and management process and shifted the focus from state control to a partnership of the state with local governments. This decision was not greeted with enthusiasm by the environmental community, many of whom were concerned that rural local governments lacked the capacity to manage development to achieve environmental protection objectives (Schoenbaum 1974). But local opposition to a completely centralized program was too strong. In fact, when Governor Holshouser initiated a companion Mountain Area Management Act (MAMA) in 1974, it was vigorously opposed by mountain legislator Liston Ramsey (who was arguably the most powerful member of the state General Assembly), and it was soundly defeated. The mountain bill was reintroduced several times over the next several years and each time met defeat due to the combined opposition of economic development and local government interests.

The Coastal Area Management Act (CAMA) was enacted in 1974. To garner local support, it placed policy-making authority in the hands of the Coastal Resources Commission (CRC), composed of fifteen members, twelve of whom are appointed by the governor from local government nominees. The act charged the state with designating and regulating areas of environmental concern and local governments, under state supervision, with planning for and regulating local land use. Through later amendments, it merged the sand dune and wetlands protection laws with the coastal program to simplify and coordinate permit decisions.

The Coastal Area Management Act's planning requirements and unique allocation of responsibilities for the coastal region were challenged immediately by a recalcitrant local government (Carteret County), which asserted that the law was an improper delegation of legislative authority to the Coastal Resources Commission and that it made an arbitrary distinction between the coast and the rest of the state. In 1978, however, the North Carolina Supreme Court upheld the coastal act, saying that it is "reasonably adapted to the special needs of the coastal region and [does] not exclude from its coverage areas that clearly should have been covered" (*Adams v N.C. Dept. of Natural and Economic Resources*). The court also rejected the county's claim that state planning guidelines constituted a taking of private property without just compensation and ruled that, contrary to the county's contention, it did not violate the constitutional guarantee against illegal searches and seizures.

The Planning Mandate

The Coastal Area Management Act requires twenty coastal counties to pre-pare comprehensive land use plans. Municipalities within those counties are encouraged to prepare their own plans. If they fail to plan, then the county must plan for them. If counties also fail to plan, CAMA authorizes the state to assume this function, which it did when Carteret County challenged the constitutionality of the legislation and refused to participate in the planning process.

In contrast with California, local land use plans must comply with state guidelines, which spell out planning procedures such as citizen participation requirements, the form of plans, and the issues localities must address in their plans. The Coastal Resources Commission and state coastal manage-ment staff review each plan for compliance. Plan updates are required every five years. The state prepares new guidelines prior to each update and has used this tool to insure that local governments attend to state policy con-cerns more or less as they arise.

Although local plans must comply with state guidelines, the Coastal Re-sources Commission has no direct way to force compliance or to force local governments to adopt any specific land use policy. But it does have four im-portant tools to induce voluntary compliance. The first of these is persua-sion. The CRC has taken pains from the beginning to work with local gov-ernments and not create unnecessary local hostility. The commission, for example, goes from county to county to listen to local concerns and ideas for plan updates, and it holds its regular meetings at different locations along the coast to facilitate participation by local citizens and officials.

A second tool used to win local support is technical and financial as-sistance. The state provides hands-on technical assistance through staff located in three regional field offices. Financial assistance also has been ample, with over $1 million in aid provided to localities to finance the origi-nal round of plan preparation. Subsequent plan updates have also been paid for, in part, through state planning grants.

A third tool is consistency requirements. Once plans are prepared, they become part of North Carolina's coastal zone management program, and the consistency rules of the federal Coastal Zone Management Program apply. Thus, the plans give local governments a means to ensure that federal and state programs operate in ways consistent with local goals and policies.

Finally, the threat of state planners in Raleigh preparing the plan has been persuasive. The state reacted swiftly to Carteret County's challenge of the legislation by mounting a vigorous legal defense of the act. As important for the future effectiveness of CAMA, however, the state also did not hesitate to use the coercive provisions of the law. State planners moved quickly to prepare the Carteret plan and then used the state-prepared plan as the basis for permit decisions regarding development in areas of environmental concern.

The Coastal Area Management Act's relatively strong approach to vertical consistency, however, is not matched by similar concern for either horizontal or internal consistency. North Carolina does not have a tradition of regional planning, and CAMA makes no provisions for intergovernmental coordination at the local level. In addition, the act's requirements for internal consistency between plans and local regulations are weak.

Linking Planning and Land Use Regulation

The Coastal Area Management Act directed the Coastal Resources Commission to identify areas of environmental concern (AECs) and gave the commission two tools to protect these areas. First, within AECs, the state demands consistency between state-approved local land use plans and local regulations. Second, the state operates a system of issuing permits for development within AECs. State staff review proposals and issue permits for so-called major projects (over twenty acres or sixty thousand square feet), while local governments are authorized to handle smaller, so-called minor projects. If localities choose not to use this power, the state administers permits for both major and minor projects. Landowners and developers who fail to obtain a permit or who violate permit conditions are subject to fines of from one hundred to one thousand dollars for each violation and imprisonment of up to sixty days, and they must restore property that has been damaged.

The Coastal Resources Commission has identified a number of areas of environmental concern, such as oceanfront and estuarine shorelines, floodplains, wetlands, and similarly sensitive areas. But in the aggregate these areas constitute only about 3 percent of the coastal zone. As a result, most local development is not subject to planning consistency requirements, and most is not subject to state-issued permits.

Approach to Natural Hazards

The Coastal Area Management Act's requirements concerning land use planning and the issuance of permits address natural hazards. State guidelines require that local plans give due consideration to hazards. Requirements have become more explicit over time, so that by 1989 all plans were required to analyze and make policy recommendations for hazard mitigation, emergency evacuation, and postdisaster recovery. From the late 1970s through the mid-1980s, the state coastal management office allocated most of its staff resources to formulating permit standards to reduce hurricane and erosion hazards along the ocean shoreline (Owens 1985). The staff developed specific rules for setbacks from the ocean, the density of development in inlet areas, hurricane-resistant construction standards, and provision of information about hazards to builders. In addition, the state does not allow shoreline hardening (e.g., seawalls) to save structures threatened by erosion.

The setback standards, which were adopted in 1979, infuriated numerous landowners when they rendered eight hundred existing oceanfront lots unbuildable. To defuse mounting political opposition, in 1981 the rule was amended to exempt low-intensity uses, to grandfather in many existing lots (so that only five hundred remained undevelopable), and to acquire for beach access property unsuitable for building. (One million dollars was appropriated for this purpose).

Evaluation of CAMA's Effectiveness

Like California's planning mandate, CAMA has not been subjected to a systematic scholarly evaluation. But the entire program and certain of its aspects have been examined from time to time. In response to controversy over the ocean setback rules, the Coastal Resources Commission staff funded an evaluation of the effect of setback requirements on land values. The study found the rules had little impact (Liner 1982).

Interviews with local officials conducted in 1977 (after completion of the first round of planning) revealed strong local support for CAMA, in sharp contrast with the initial opposition of local officials to state-mandated planning (Burby 1979). The local support was reflected in the legislature several years later. In 1982, a committee of the state General Assembly reviewed

CAMA, as required by state sunset laws. Although dominated by coastal legislators, many of whom opposed initial passage of the legislation in 1974, after extensive hearings the committee gave the program a strong endorsement. In response, the 1983 legislature removed the sunset provision and
quadrupled state funding to make up for federal cutbacks in the coastal zone
management program (Owens 1985).

Finally, a study on permit compliance found that the conditions attached
to most permits seemed to be sufficient to conserve natural resources. But
the researchers found that shortfalls in compliance with permit conditions
were widespread, in part because the staff lacked resources for monitoring
and inspection (Brower and Ballenger 1991).

Attempts to Make Governments Plan Statewide

At the same time it created the coastal area management program, the
North Carolina legislature established a state land policy council to examine
the need for statewide growth management and planning. In 1976, the land
policy council issued its final report. The council called for legislation to
mandate planning statewide in keeping with proposed state growth management goals and policies (North Carolina Land Policy Council 1976). Legislation to implement the recommendations of the council was subsequently introduced in 1977, but when newly elected Democratic governor James Hunt
gave it only lukewarm support, it made little progress in the General Assembly, and it drew fire from local governments and entrenched agricultural
and forestry interests (DeGrove 1984).

The defeat of the land policy council recommendations, along with a similar drubbing given to a proposed Mountain Area Management Act in the
1974, 1975, and 1976 sessions of the legislature, killed state interest in land
use planning legislation for fifteen years. But with action on land use issues
occurring in nearby Georgia, Maryland, and Virginia in the latter half of the
1980s, North Carolina legislators began to take note. The 1991 General Assembly passed a bill forming a Legislative Study Commission to examine op-
tions for statewide comprehensive planning. The commission held hearings
annually between 1992 and 1995, but no new legislation was forthcoming.

Single-Purpose Mandates

North Carolina has relatively few single-purpose mandates that affect local
government planning for hazard mitigation. As reported above, shortly after

CAMA was adopted the state merged wetlands and sand dune protection laws into the coastal program. In 1971, in response to the National Flood Insurance Program, North Carolina adopted a floodway act that called upon local governments to adopt ordinances to prevent the obstruction of floodways. Local regulations were not mandated, and no deadline for local action was prescribed. The weaknesses in the floodway act led one official to assert a few years later that "North Carolina does not have a floodplain management program" (quoted in Burby 1977, 20). The deficiencies in the floodway law were subsequently dealt with by the state building code, which is the only noteworthy single-purpose mandate drawing local governmental attention to hazard mitigation.

North Carolina has established uniform statewide building standards for design and construction materials and practices and a certification process for local building inspectors. The standards address wind, flood, and seismic forces, and beginning in 1995, the code will be updated every three years. Strict structural standards to prevent damage from high winds apply in the coastal zone. The standards for building design to prevent damage from flooding are consistent with the National Flood Insurance Program, and the standards to minimize damage from earthquakes apply to the more seismically active western portion of the state. The code regulates all public and private construction with exemptions for certain types of agricultural buildings. If builders do not comply with the requirements, they are subject to penalties including stop-work orders, permit revocation, compliance orders, fines, and judicial action.

The state's earliest efforts to regulate building practices and maintenance focused on the preservation of healthy and sanitary conditions and the avoidance of fire. A 1905 state law required local building inspection in jurisdictions with populations over one thousand. North Carolina's first statewide building code was written by the state Building Code Council, which was made up of professionals in the field, and ratified by the General Assembly in 1941. The Building Code Council continues to administer the code.

In 1969, the state required cities and counties to create inspection departments. To improve the quality of building inspection, a Code Officials Qualification Board was established in 1977, and local governments were prohibited from issuing permits without appropriately certified inspectors. The statute provides that the state retains the ability to reassert authority over inspections if local compliance is deemed inadequate, and the state may sanction local inspectors directly by removing their certification or through criminal proceedings.

The Building Code Council membership, still drawn primarily from the construction industry, is appointed by the governor. The construction industry has continued to be supportive of the codes. In 1969, manufacturers of mobile homes attempted to exempt mobile homes from the code's coverage, but Building Code Council officials resisted this exemption, and it was never granted. Given the widespread use of mobile homes in North Carolina and their susceptibility to hazards such as coastal storms and hurricanes, the defeat of this exemption was a particularly important component of North Carolina's hazard mitigation effort.

Concluding Note

The North Carolina planning mandate, although not applied statewide, is typical of a number of advances in the design of state planning mandates made during the early 1970s. At this time, states stepped forward and asserted the primacy of state land use goals, especially concerning environmental quality. State oversight of local government planning moved from enabling plan making to requiring plans and specifying how they are to be prepared. At the same time, many of these 1970s state programs were designed in the face of stiff opposition from local governments and strong skepticism on the part of environmentalists about whether local governments had the capacity and the will to manage land use to protect critical natural values. The legislation that resulted from these two concerns has a dual personality. It is strong in forcing environmental concerns on local government and retaining at the state level the power to issue permits for development in environmentally sensitive areas. But it is weak in forcing other state policy concerns onto local planning agendas and in requiring high-quality, truly comprehensive local plans. The legislation, as it unfolded in North Carolina, is weak in one other respect. It gives scant attention to the extralocal effects of local land use decisions. Nowhere in the CAMA legislation or administrative rule making can one find any attention to regional cooperation and coordination of land use policy beyond the level of individual counties.

In spite of its shortcomings, CAMA stands as an exemplar of a substate approach to planning mandates and of a concerted attempt by the state to merge into one program an array of previously single-purpose state environmental permits. By maintaining a balance between state and local interests, it has managed to survive politically and, if anything, to garner increased legislative and local popular support over more than two decades.

4

Florida
Putting It All Together

Florida was at the forefront of state growth management in the 1970s. Learning from early missteps, in 1985 state policy makers completely revamped Florida's planning legislation. The revised approach features strong state direction of planning and regulation to accomplish clearly specified state goals. Florida's planning mandate pays attention to horizontal consistency by requiring local plans and policies to conform to regional plans. Internal consistency is demanded as well. Land use regulations and investments in capital improvements must conform to policies spelled out in the local plan, and development cannot be allowed if it will outstrip the available capacity of urban infrastructure.

Florida has literally "put it all together" by including in its growth management legislation each of the prescriptions planning theorists believe will produce an effective state and local development management effort. At the same time, Florida's policy makers learned a key point: strong state laws that lack adequate monitoring and enforcement mechanisms frequently founder. In its new approach, Florida added teeth to its program, so that local governments are punished if they ignore state policy prescriptions. It accompanied these sanctions with significant rewards for compliance, to induce local governments to willingly follow the state lead. In this chapter, we trace the evolution of this innovative scheme and also describe how Florida reinforces its planning mandate with a variety of single-purpose programs aimed specifically at hazard mitigation.

Setting the Stage

Historically poor and sparsely settled, Florida has witnessed repeated attempts to convert the state's assets—its mild climate, beauty, and natural resources—into growth and economic prosperity. Faced with a landscape dominated in the south by swamps and coastal marshes, state and federal agencies offered numerous incentives to drain, dredge, fill, and otherwise transform this supposedly unproductive terrain into dry land suitable for building. Florida's drive to entice in-migration paid dividends after World War II, when the state experienced an enormous surge in urban growth. From a population of less than 3 million in 1950, the state grew by almost 6 million over the next twenty-five years, moving it from the twentieth to the eighth largest state. By the time of the 1990 census, the population had topped 13 million, and state forecasters projected that number would double to 26 million by 2020 (DeGrove 1990). Florida's population explosion created enormous wealth, but it also placed severe strains on natural resources and physical infrastructure such as transportation and water and sewerage systems.

In particular, millions of people in Florida are at risk from natural hazards. Florida contains a vast system of wetlands (they cover a third of the state), so that growth has been concentrated in low-lying areas near the coast. The Federal Emergency Management Agency estimated in 1991 that over ten thousand square miles in Florida are prone to flooding, with over 1 million households and $46 billion in property located in areas vulnerable to flooding from a hundred-year storm (L. R. Johnston Associates 1992). Between 1982 and 1992, storms resulted in seven presidential disaster declarations involving thirty-four of the state's sixty-seven counties. Hurricane winds may pose an even greater threat. Flooding caused relatively little damage when Hurricane Andrew came ashore in August 1992, but winds that gusted to almost 200 mph produced some $20 billion in losses (Interagency Hazard Mitigation Team 1992).

Andrew brought home once again the problems created by massive urban development in ecologically fragile and vulnerable environments. Many of these problems tend to be concentrated in the southern part of the state. By the 1960s, crises in the water supply had become annual events, muck fires burned out of control in the Everglades, saltwater intruded into the potable water supplies, bays and estuaries had been fouled by inadequate sewage treatment, and virtually every square inch of dry (and wet) land was being subdivided and sold to northerners hungry for a warm place to live (McCluney 1971).

Environmental problems produced widespread concern, but citizen environmental activism came to a head over two bellwether events in the late 1960s: the proposal by the Corps of Engineers to build a barge canal across the state and the Dade County Port Authority proposal to locate a regional jetport in the Big Cypress Swamp west of Miami (Blackwelder 1972). Both proposals were beaten back, but only after long, contentious political battles. Those struggles to protect Florida's environment provided a training ground for the interest groups and legislators who eventually played a leading role in the formulation and passage of a state growth management program (see DeGrove 1984).

The First Generation of State Planning Mandates

When the public began to demand action on environmental problems, local planning staffs were ill equipped to respond with aggressive growth management programs. As late as 1967, some Florida counties lacked the power to regulate land use, and less than half had in place any form of land use regulation (Bartley 1973). At the state level, some single-purpose legislation had been enacted to stem mounting water and air pollution, shoreline erosion, and dredging and filling and to foster historic preservation. But by the early 1970s, it was evident that this piecemeal approach was not keeping up with the pressures continued rapid growth placed on environmental resources and public infrastructure (deHaven-Smith 1984).

The need for a greater state role in growth management became self-evident following a severe drought in 1970 and 1971 (Carter 1975). In search of a solution to the water shortage, Governor Reuben Askew convened a conference in 1971 on water management in South Florida. The conferees considered solutions to water supply problems, but they went further and addressed the broader problem of managing growth. Askew then created the Task Force on Resource Management to develop legislation to carry out the conference recommendations. Four bills were proposed: the Florida State Comprehensive Planning Act, the Environmental Land and Water Management Act, the Land Conservation Act, and the Florida Water Resources Act.

In crafting the comprehensive-planning legislation, the task force hoped to create a well-coordinated state growth management program. The other three bills (discussed later with other single-purpose legislation) addressed specific growth management issues, including protection of environmentally sensitive areas, consideration of the regional impacts of development in local land use decision making, and correction of long-standing flood control and drainage problems. By the end of the 1972 legislative session, sustained media attention, strong legislative and gubernatorial leadership, and effective lobbying by groups such as the League of Women Voters and a major development corporation (Arvida) had secured passage of each bill (DeGrove 1984; Pelham 1979).

The comprehensive planning act sought to strengthen planning and program coordination in state government by creating a Division of State Planning in the Department of Administration, which was to coordinate preparation of a state development plan. However, this program was "virtual[ly] stillborn" (Wallis 1993, 5), and it never resulted in a useful state comprehensive plan. According to political scientist Lance deHaven-Smith (1984), the plan produced was too long and the goals and policies it contained too vague and contradictory to serve as guides to land use planning by state, regional, or local governments. The plan did not mandate action on its recommendations but was merely advisory, and, as a result, state and regional agencies generally ignored its suggestions (see DeGrove 1984).

Mandated local planning, consistent with state goals, was part of the proposed 1972 legislation. When that drew strong opposition from local governments, the idea was dropped. After the 1972 session, Governor Askew appointed a study commission (the Environmental Land and Water Management Study Committee) to find ways to coordinate state and local policy. The committee approached the 1974 session of the state legislature with another bill mandating local planning. To make the legislation more acceptable to local governments, it included financial assistance to cities and counties to prepare the required plans. The incentives offered were not large enough to persuade localities to accept state interference in their planning, and this bill met continued strong opposition from local governments and ultimately failed (Healy 1976). By 1975, however, continuing problems traceable to urban growth made the need for local land use planning more evident than ever, and the legislature bit the bullet and passed the Local Government Comprehensive Planning Act. This legislation required local adoption and implementation of comprehensive plans. If local officials failed to plan within four years, the act authorized county governments or the state to plan for them (Jackson 1979). But aside from an advisory regional and state review, no teeth were provided to ensure that plans addressed important state or regional goals or met minimal standards for plan quality, and no funds were provided to help local governments prepare the plans the state demanded.

The state planning mandate received little support from local government officials. The plans it spawned varied widely in quality. And without a means for the state to enforce internal consistency (which the legislation required), local land development regulations and development orders frequently ignored the policies proposed in land use plans. Lance deHaven-Smith summed up the system's failure thus:

> Lacking clear state and regional policy, Florida's growth-management system has evolved strong thumbs but weak fingers. . . . The system's weak fingers are at the local level in the planning, amendment, and review process. Plans exert very little influence over local land-use regulation. When there is a conflict between the plan and a desired zoning decision, it is often the plan rather than the zoning decision that is adjusted. Many local governments amend their comprehensive plans as often as every few weeks. . . .[Required] regional and state review [are] simply circumvented. (deHaven-Smith 1984, 417)

By the early 1980s, these deficiencies were so glaring that growth management advocates mounted a second campaign to craft an effective state planning program.

The Second Generation of Planning Mandates

In 1982, Governor Bob Graham formed the second Environmental Land Management Study Committee (ELMS II), composed of a cross section of interests concerned with growth management issues, and told the committee to evaluate Florida's planning system. In its 1984 final report, the members of ELMS II concluded that funding and enforcement were deficient, the system lacked overall policy guidance and coordination, and local planning alone was insufficient to ensure effective growth management. It recommended a statewide planning framework anchored by a legislatively adopted state plan. To improve implementation, the committee recommended that citizens be given standing to enforce the growth management scheme and that adequate funding for planning be provided. Finally, it recommended strengthening coastal management by increasing funding to protect coastal resources, requiring state approval of the coastal protection elements of local plans, and implementing state regulations to protect critical areas.

State and Regional Planning Mandates

The State and Regional Planning Act of 1984 was the first legislative response to the recommendations of ELMS II. The law mandated the preparation of a state comprehensive plan by the governor's office, which was to be presented to the legislature for adoption in 1985. It also required the preparation and adoption of state agency functional plans and regional comprehensive plans, each to be consistent with the overall state plan (Pelham, Hyde, and Banks 1985). A first-time appropriation of $500,000 to the state's eleven regional planning councils supported the initial work on regional plans. The initial grant was supplemented by $2 million in additional funds over the next two years, so that by 1987 all eleven regional plans had been prepared.

The governor's office presented the proposed state plan to the 1985 legislature after holding extensive public hearings, and the legislature passed the State Comprehensive Planning Act early in the session by a strong majority in both houses. The new state plan was reasonably concise but also comprehensive, containing twenty-seven goals and accompanying policies, including goals and policies dealing with public safety. Since its adoption, the plan has served as the cornerstone of Florida's growth management system.

The New Local Planning Mandate

The integrated policy framework sought by growth management advocates was finally put in place by passage of the second major law in 1985: the Omnibus Growth Management Act. One part of the omnibus law, the Local Government Comprehensive Planning and Land Development Regulation Act, mandated new local comprehensive plans and required that they be consistent with the goals of the state plan, the comprehensive regional policy plans, and other applicable statutes. It authorized the state to establish minimum criteria for local plans, which the Department of Community Affairs subsequently acted on through Rule 9J-5 of the Florida Administrative Code. This requirement for vertical consistency is complemented by horizontal consistency requirements. Each local plan must include an intergovernmental element so that all local plans in a region are compatible with one another. Local plan elements also must be consistent with one another, a requirement that is important for hazard mitigation, since hurricane evacuation routes can be protected from overdevelopment by the requirement that the traffic circulation, coastal, and future land use elements of local plans be coordinated and mutually consistent.

Rule 9J-5 and Natural Hazards

The broad mandates of the growth management act are given shape and substance by Rule 9J-5, which sets minimum standards for judging the adequacy of local plans submitted for state approval. Rule 9J-5 requires certain elements in local plans and prescribes methods local governments must use in preparing plans. Element by element, it lists the types of data, issues, goals, and objectives that must be addressed, in almost a checklist format. It also requires specific, measurable objectives that can be used by the state to monitor local government progress in meeting state goals.

The rule addressed natural hazards in the required coastal management element. Coastal management provisions of local plans must: (1) limit public expenditures that subsidize development in high-hazard areas unless the expenditures are related to restoration and enhancement of natural resources; (2) direct population concentrations away from known or predicted high-hazard areas; (3) maintain or reduce hurricane evacuation times; and (4) include postdisaster redevelopment plans to reduce exposure of human life and property to natural hazards. These requirements signal a complete reversal of policy in a state that in the 1950s and 1960s was infamous for allowing wholesale subdivision and marketing of property that was not only prone to flooding but often actually permanently under water!

In addition to the required coastal element, hurricane and natural disaster considerations are addressed in other components of the general comprehensive-planning process. Floodplain management has to be considered in the future land use, conservation, and coastal management elements of comprehensive plans and also in land development regulations. Rule 9J-5 defined floodplains as areas that would be inundated during a hundred-year-flood event, the same standard used by the National Flood Insurance Program.

Implementing the New Planning Requirements

The Department of Community Affairs adopted similar rules to implement other portions of the growth management legislation (DeGrove and Stroud 1987). For instance, Rule 9J-12 established an enforceable schedule of due dates for all local plans. Rules 9J-5.0055 and 9J-24 provided guidance for meeting the concurrency requirement that public facilities and services be adequate to meet the needs of new development. While the concurrency provision does not deal directly with hazards, it does control the extent to which overburdened, older, usually coastal areas of Florida can continue to grow. For example, an amendment to the Collier County comprehensive plan was rejected because by lowering the level of service standards of its traffic circulation element, it would have permitted a hurricane evacuation route to become too congested. Both the state and the Treasure Coast Regional Planning Council objected, and Collier County eventually withdrew the proposal.

The Department of Community Affairs also tried to influence the shape of local plans and regulations through model comprehensive-plan elements and a model land development code for a mythical Florida city. The conservation and future land use elements address planning for floodplains, and the coastal management element includes a plan for hurricane evacuation. The department disseminates two additional technical aids: a newsletter with advice on compliance and copies of plan evaluations that highlight sections of plans the department has rejected because they are not in compliance with Rule 9J-5. In the staff's opinion, the newsletter is an invaluable tool for educating local planners about the process and about the department's evolving substantive interpretations of Rule 9J-5 and the growth management law.

The rules, as a whole, were very successful in getting the act implemented in a relatively short period of time. Within six years of its enactment, all 457 required city and county comprehensive plans (and most land development regulations) had been adopted. However, only 186 plans were in complete compliance when originally submitted for review. The remainder had problems that required state officials to go back to local officials and negotiate a mutually satisfactory resolution, which was cemented by state issuance of an administrative compliance agreement.

The state's plan review focused on a number of important issues that directly affected hazard mitigation, such as the level of development allowed on barrier islands and in coastal high-hazard areas. Failure to deal adequately with natural hazards led the state to reject several local plans upon original submission, and the state rejected plan amendments that would have allowed development to employ less stringent standards regarding the hundred-year-storm event.

Like North Carolina's and unlike California's, Florida's growth management law requires plans to be periodically revised and updated. Rule 9J-12 established an enforceable schedule of completion dates for all local plans. Amendments to adopted plans cannot occur more frequently than twice a year, and each amendment is subject to review by the state for consistency with state policy. At least once every seven years, local plans must be formally evaluated by the locality and then amended to put in place any necessary changes. These updates, termed Evaluation and Appraisal Reports (EARs, in Florida planning jargon), must incorporate changes in state and regional policy that have occurred during the interim period as well as respond to changes in community circumstances brought about by growth,

decline, or other factors. The Department of Community Affairs is authorized to review the adequacy of the local plan update process, including required citizen participation, and to review proposed amendments to local
plans to ensure that they are consistent with state and regional policy.

In Rule 9J-11, the state carefully specified the procedures all parties are
to follow in preparing and amending comprehensive plans. The state process for reviewing local plans for compliance with state standards is highly
prescriptive. It assures that all parties with a stake in the outcome of planning decisions have an opportunity to be heard. The growth management
legislation specifically requires citizen participation in the process of preparing land use plans, and it gives citizens the right to intervene if they believe
that local planning or regulatory decisions contravene state policy. In addition, if a local government fails to adopt a required land use regulation, the
Department of Community Affairs may bring an enforcement action in the
Florida trial courts to compel compliance.

In reviewing local comprehensive plans and land use regulations for consistency with state standards, the Department of Community Affairs early
on signaled its serious intent to require compliance with hazard mitigation
requirements. In 1991, it rejected the City of Jacksonville/Duvall County's
comprehensive plan, in part because it failed to meet state standards for
floodplain management and protection of coastal resources. Another community adopted a plan that would have overloaded evacuation routes in the
event of a hurricane emergency; in response, the state rejected the plan and
recommended that the locality reduce proposed development densities and
intensities. Finally, it has also held local governments to a strict definition of
hazardous areas. When the City of Lynn Haven sought to amend its plan to
allow development in a high-hazard area by relaxing its definition of areas at
risk from hurricane hazards, the state rejected the amendment.

Offering a Carrot and Wielding the Stick

One of the keys to the high degree of compliance attained in Florida is the
significant leverage (both carrots and sticks) the growth management legislation puts in the hands of state officials. The carrots consist of significant technical and financial assistance both to build local government capacity to plan
and to lower costs to comply with state requirements. Those measures also
serve to reduce political opposition and have kept to a minimum local efforts
to repeal the program.

The Department of Community Affairs has worked to improve the capacity of local governments to plan for and manage development by formu-

lating and disseminating model comprehensive-plan elements and a model land development code for a mythical Florida city. The elements relating to conservation and future land use address planning for floodplains, and the coastal management element includes a plan for hurricane evacuation. Technical assistance provided local governments by the Department of Community Affairs is supplemented by technical assistance from the eleven regional planning agencies.

Florida has provided significant financial assistance to help local governments prepare comprehensive plans and bring land use and other regulations into conformity with local plans and state growth management policies. Between 1985 and 1993, the state provided local governments with a total of $36 million in planning grants, approximately 4 percent of the $909 million in total local planning costs over that period. In fiscal year 1994, no new grants were made, since by then all of the required local comprehensive plans had been prepared, but the governor requested an additional $2.5 million to cover new costs imposed by legislation in 1993 that requires local governments to revise their comprehensive plans so that they are consistent with state policy.

The sticks include sanctions the Florida legislature authorized for local governments that did not submit plans on time and for plans found not in compliance with the growth management act. The governor and the cabinet, sitting as the Florida Administration Commission, established policies for imposing sanctions at the end of 1989. The Department of Community Affairs has the ultimate authority to determine the consistency of local plans with both state and regional requirements. The state can withhold $\frac{1}{365}$ of state revenue-sharing funds for each day a plan is late or held to be out of compliance. This sanction has been challenged, but it was upheld by the Florida courts (*Florida League of Cities, Inc., v Administration Commission*).

For the most part, however, rather than vigorously imposing sanctions Florida state officials have used them more as threat to gain leverage in negotiating compliance with state standards. By using the plan compliance agreement mechanism, the state has been successful in keeping litigation in the state courts to a minimum (DeGrove 1992).

Fine Tuning the Growth Management System

The legislature did not tamper with the planning scheme from 1986 to 1991. A Growth Management Task Force established by Governor Lawton Chiles examined the system in 1991 and prepared recommendations for its improvement. The task force found that the weakest link in the state's comprehensive-planning scheme was the state. Governor Bob Martinez, who preceded Chiles, supported growth management but was not willing to provide the leadership to bring state agencies into line. The governor's office never completed the various components of the state comprehensive plan that were designed to link budgeting with planning at the state level. The task force also found that the governor had failed to provide executive leadership in updating the state comprehensive-plan goals and objectives and in coordinating the various agency plans (Florida Governor's Growth Management Transition Team Task Force 1991).

A number of proposed bills that would weaken the system cleared legislative committees in 1992 and even appeared to come close to passage. With one exception, all failed. The support they received was a clear sign of legislative frustration with the system in the face of a failure to fund growth management adequately. A bill to abolish regional planning councils in 1993, unless they were reauthorized by each chamber in the 1993 session of the legislature, passed by an overwhelming margin over strong objections by the state American Planning Association Chapter, 1000 Friends of Florida, and other supporters of growth management and was allowed by the governor to become law. Regional planning was reauthorized in 1993, but this law was indicative of weaknesses in public and political support for the middle level in the system. The silence of Florida's League of Cities and Association of Counties while the bill was being debated doubtless helped it to pass.

In contrast with those efforts to scuttle or weaken state growth management, a fine-tuning bill, supported by the Department of Community Affairs, was enacted in 1992. In the words of a 1000 Friends of Florida newsletter, the bill "puts the compliance review process into the law, encourages innovative urban and regional planning policies, [and] sets up an alternative [and simpler] procedure for amending comprehensive plans" (cited in DeGrove 1992, 28). The law also extended by a year the 1993 deadline for beginning local submission of Evaluation and Appraisal Reports to enable the Department of Community Affairs to prepare adequately for the next round of plan reviews.

Governor Chiles named a third Environmental and Land Management Study Committee in 1991. The committee issued its final report in December 1992, and the legislature enacted many of its recommendations on the final day (May 11) of the 1993 legislative session. Among its various provisions, the bill ELMS III proposed (1) required review and revision of the state comprehensive plan every two years; (2) directed regional planning councils to prepare strategic regional plans (rather than regional policy plans) to carry out the state comprehensive plan; (3) streamlined the process for state review of proposed plan amendments; and (4) strengthened requirements for intergovernmental coordination. The latter requires local plans to demonstrate that they are consistent with and further the state comprehensive plan and their regional policy plan and to demonstrate that consideration has been given to the impact of the plan on the development of adjacent jurisdictions.

Possibly the most serious challenge to growth management in Florida came in 1995, when, responding to a national movement to soften the impact of regulations on landowners, the legislature adopted the Private Property Rights Protection Act. Section 1 of the act creates a new cause of action against governments that impose an "inordinate burden" on real property by restricting either the existing use of property or its prospective use. However, because this provision applies only to governmental acts after May 11, 1995, it does not affect previous growth management legislation. This provision, together with other limitations on the relief afforded landowners, led a group of legal experts to conclude, "The new law grants important new rights and remedies to landowners while protecting existing environmental and growth management programs" (Powell, Rhodes, and Stengle 1995, 11).

Evaluation of the Planning Legislation

While the growth management program survived judicial scrutiny and careful review by ELMS III and the state legislature, it did less well in an evaluation by planning educators from Florida State University. Focusing specifically on hurricane hazard mitigation, professors Robert Deyle and Richard Smith examined the coastal management elements of eighteen local plans. They concluded that

> many local plans do not meet the intent of the state's planning mandates. No single community was found to meet all of the 9J-5 requirements, and in many instances the requirements were met only with broad and general statements referencing an intent to consider a policy at some future date. Similarly, where requirements were deemed to be met they often were done so in language that was vague or by references to ordinances and regulations whose content was left unspecified. Most plans, moreover, were found to be uncreative; they often included simple and common regulatory mechanisms . . . but lacked policies that go beyond basic regulation. . . . We conclude from this review of local coastal plans that the system of translating state policy objectives for hazard mitigation to localities is not working well and that considerable leverage for the purpose of achieving state policy objectives has been lost. (Deyle and Smith 1994, 196)

This is harsh criticism of a program that many observers rate as the most stringent planning mandate in the United States.

Single-Purpose Mandates

The hazard mitigation standards of the growth management legislation are supplemented by a number of single-purpose laws. These include regulation of shoreline development, establishment of regional flood control agencies, state standards for local building codes, a state-supervised system of permit administration for large developments with likely regional impacts, and a program to manage development in large, environmentally sensitive areas. Here we review each of these briefly with an eye on the efforts of local governments to manage development and mitigate losses from natural hazards.

Beach and Shoreline Preservation

The Beach and Shoreline Preservation Act of 1965 created a Beach Management Trust Fund to finance beach management planning and preservation for up to 75 percent of the cost of beach restoration, beach nourishment, and hurricane protection. The act gives the governor the power to declare a shore erosion emergency, which can free up additional funds to alleviate erosion. County beach and shore preservation districts are authorized to carry out local beach management planning and given a limited ability to levy ad valorem taxes and issue bonds.

In addition to, and more significant than, the state aid it provided, the Beach and Shoreline Preservation Act also inserted state authority into decision making about shoreline development. It created a program administered by the Department of Natural Resources that issues permits for construction below the mean high-water line of tidal waters. Construction on sandy beaches is prohibited within fifty feet of the mean high-water line or any erosion control line established landward of the mean high-water line. Local governments are required to notify the department of local permit applications covered by the act and to notify the applicant of the state requirements. In 1971, the act was amended to also require local governments to impose additional and more-stringent building standards seaward of a coastal construction control line, which is based on anticipated erosion rates and designed to include all the area subject to a hundred-year-hurricane storm surge. In addition to providing protection against coastal storms, the required coastal construction setback lines insure that development does not interfere with natural shoreline fluctuations or dune stability and recovery following storm events. While delegating administrative duties to local governments, the Department of Natural Resources retains the right of final approval when any deviation from its standards is proposed and the right to reassert administrative control, if required.

The 1985 Growth Management Act amended the Beach and Shoreline Preservation Act to strengthen its provisions and coordinate its application with local comprehensive plans. The amendments specifically recognize the value of the beach dune system as the first line of defense for the mainland against winter storms and hurricanes, the increased risks created by construction in these areas, and the considerable cost to the state associated with postdisaster redevelopment. The growth management amendments created a new coastal building zone, larger than the area previously regulated by the Beach and Shoreline Preservation Act. Development within the zone is categorized as either minor (expendable in the event of a storm) or major. Habitable major structures must comply with the state building code and the regulations of the National Flood Insurance Program and be able to withstand at least 110-mph winds. The zone includes all coastal barrier islands and the Florida Keys. The area between the seasonal high-water line and fifteen hundred feet landward of the coastal construction control line (or three thousand feet landward of the mean high-water line in the absence of a coastal construction control line) is also included in the coastal building zone.

A new construction prohibition zone was created. This zone includes the area seaward of the seasonal high-water line predicted for the next thirty years. The Department of Natural Resources cannot issue permits for development within this zone, and the restrictions on building must be disclosed when property is sold.

The growth management act built upon Executive Order 81–105 by prohibiting state funding for bridging previously unbridged barrier islands and any increase in local infrastructure capacity in ways inconsistent with local comprehensive plans. This order, originally adopted by Governor Graham in 1981, had placed limits on the use of state funds to ease development on barrier islands if evacuation times were greater than twelve hours or new development would lead to excessive (greater than twelve-hour) evacuation times. While intended to restrict the use of state funds for posthurricane reconstruction, the order proved difficult to interpret and enforce. The 1985 growth management legislation remedied these problems.

The growth management act also allowed the state to refuse to include local projects in its applications for Federal Emergency Management Agency

disaster assistance unless the local government previously adopted or con-
tractually obligated itself to adopt a hazard mitigation plan (before the disaster) addressing building codes, flooding, public infrastructure, public information systems, preventive planning measures to ameliorate potential storm
damage, and the ability of certain land uses to locate or be reconstructed in
coastal high-hazard areas.

Controlling Floods

The Water Resources Act, another one of the environmental programs enacted in 1972, created a system of five regional water management districts
to deal with flooding and other water resources issues. The districts operate
under the loose supervision of the state Department of Environmental
Regulation, but they were established as special districts with taxing powers
and independent governing boards appointed by the governor. District
boundaries are coterminous with those of the state's major watersheds. The
districts are responsible for flood control, own and manage Florida's extensive system of drainage works, and manage the consumptive use of water resources through a system of permits. Over time, the emphasis of the districts
has shifted from engineering flood control works to more-explicit management of water resources to balance the competing needs of agriculture, the
environment, and urban areas.

No systematic studies have been conducted on the impacts of the water
management districts on local government attention to hazard mitigation.
The Joint Center for Urban and Environmental Problems at Florida Atlantic
University/Florida International University examined floodplain management issues in the state. The center's study concluded that many local governments were locked into a "drain and ditch" mentality and were "shrug-
ging off floodplain management as either an occasionally irritating local
drainage issue or pawning the issue off as a WMD [water management dis-
trict] problem" (Paterson 1988, 16). Thus, it seems possible that the creation
of regional water management agencies could suppress local government attention to flood hazard mitigation.

Minimizing Risks to Buildings

The Florida Building Codes Act of 1974 created the State Minimum Building Code. The code includes references to several nationally recognized
model codes that may be relied on in meeting state requirements. Most
cities and counties have adopted the Standard Building Code created by the

Southern Building Code Congress International, Inc., although a few use the South Florida Building Code, created by the Dade County Board of Commissioners.

There were no special state requirements for building in coastal areas until enactment of the Coastal Zone Protection Act of 1985. This act imposes stricter building standards in specified areas to minimize damage to the environment, property, and life. As noted earlier, Florida's coastal building zone is defined in most places as the area from the seasonal high-water line to a line fifteen hundred feet landward of the coastal construction control line. Within this zone, structures must comply with minimum National Flood Insurance Program regulations. Major structures must also be designed and constructed to withstand specified minimum wind velocities in accordance with the 1986 revisions to the Standard Building Code—up to 110 mph (115 mph in the Florida Keys). The Coastal Zone Protection Act is administered and enforced by local governments. State involvement, through the Department of Natural Resources, is limited to providing technical assistance and enforcing compliance by local governments (Florida Department of Community Affairs 1986; Deyle and Smith 1994).

The failure of thousands of structures in south Dade County during Hurricane Andrew raised a public outcry about the ineffectiveness of building codes. Andrew, a focused Category 4 storm that cut a swath of destruction through south Dade County, resulted in an estimated $20 billion in property damage. Poststorm analysis revealed three major causes for the widespread destruction: (1) the force of the winds themselves, estimated to involve sustained speeds between 140 and 160 mph with gusts as high as 200 mph; (2) a weakening of adopted building codes through modifications and exceptions granted on a piecemeal basis by the Dade County Board of Commissioners; and (3) a persistent understaffing and undertraining of county code enforcement personnel (Interagency Hazard Mitigation Team 1992).

Regulating Large Projects and Sensitive Areas

The Environmental Land and Water Management Act, one of the package of growth management laws enacted in 1972, delineated the types of development and environmentally sensitive areas over which the state chose to assert special planning and regulatory authority. The act employed two concepts embodied in the American Law Institute's Model Land Development Code. The first, the Development of Regional Impact (DRI) program, applies to developments having a substantial effect on the health, safety, or welfare of the citizens of more than one county. The second, the Areas of

Critical State Concern program, provides a process for identifying and then protecting important sensitive environments.

The DRI program relies primarily on developers to initiate projects for review. The role of the state is to identify which projects are covered by the program and to provide supervision. Florida's eleven regional planning councils prepare reports and recommendations to local governments about the regional environmental, social, and economic impacts of proposed large projects. These reviews include considerations related to public safety. Legislation enacted in 1993 sharply curtailed the role of regional agencies in the DRI review process. Local governments are charged with examining the consistency of the projects with local plans, local land development regulations, and the regional planning council recommendations (until 1993) and then making a final decision whether to approve the project. The state, regional planning councils, and developer have the right to appeal local government decisions to the governor and the cabinet, sitting as the Land and Water Adjudicatory Commission.

The Areas of Critical State Concern program is designed to protect areas deemed to have statewide environmental, historical, natural, archaeological, or other importance; areas can be nominated by any person or group. The program provides two approaches to protect areas of state concern. With the first, local governments can volunteer to prepare a management plan by establishing a Resource Planning and Management Committee. However, if that voluntary plan does not address the state's concerns, the second approach can be invoked with designation of an area of critical state concern by the governor and the cabinet, sitting as the Florida Administration Commission. Once designated, local governments are given six months to create land use regulations that address state and regional concerns and follow the state planning agency's recommendation. The local effort can be rejected or amended by the state, and if the local government chooses not to act, the statute directs the state planning agency to adopt regulations for it. The state planning agency retains its power to review and modify any later local government regulatory action in a designated area of critical state concern.

Since 1972, four areas have been so designated: Big Cypress Swamp, Green Swamp, the Florida Keys, and Apalachicola Bay (in Franklin County). Hurricane hazard mitigation has been a major concern in the Florida Keys area of critical state concern. The Monroe County (which contains the Florida Keys) comprehensive plan uses evacuation time as the key limiting factor in determining how much new development can be accommodated in the Keys. Management plans have been prepared by eight other Resource Planning and Management Committees, and all focus in part on hurricane hazards and floodplain management. These plans cover large areas of Florida's coasts and the floodplains of important rivers (DeGrove and deHaven-Smith 1987).

Concluding Note

The single-purpose, environment-focused programs put in place by Florida's policy makers in the 1960s and 1970s contained many of the pieces needed for growth management. But at that time Florida's planning mandate was sorely deficient because it offered no incentives for local governments to plan and had only weak sanctions to help build their commitment to planning. While some planning took place where environmental interests had gained power, many local governments continued to foster growth indiscriminately while generally ignoring the adverse consequences of growth. To many observers, however, the most serious flaw of the old system was lack of adequate specification of what the state wanted to see in local comprehensive plans. Without a state plan, there was little basis for state review of local plans or policy guidance to regional councils in their review of large-scale development projects.

The reforms enacted between 1984 and 1986 corrected this deficiency by putting in place a state plan to provide policy guidance and then, through Rule 9J-5, a long list of detailed specifications for the content of local plans. Where the previous system had paid little attention to building the capacity of local governments to plan and manage growth, the new one provided a number of grant-in-aid programs to foster local planning. In addition, a large staff in the Department of Community Affairs was created to provide technical assistance for the planning efforts. Over time, Florida's policy makers replaced a generally weak planning system with a strong program to both plan for and manage urban development in ways consistent with state policy objectives.

5

Texas and Washington
Marching to a Different Drummer

Although facing growth and environmental problems similar to the other states in our study, Texas and Washington decided to limit state intervention to a few single-purpose mandates aimed at specific environmental problems. Of the two states, Texas has been particularly circumspect in imposing state requirements on either local governments or the private sector. Washington has not been hesitant to regulate land use, but prior to 1990 it steered clear of broad growth management legislation. In response to a strong property rights ethos and stiff opposition to state regulation from the oil and gas industry, Texas generally left development management decisions to local government. In response to a strong populist tradition and city and county opposition to state interference in local affairs, Washington was more responsive to citizen concerns, enacting a variety of laws to protect environmental quality.

Texas: A Minimalist Approach

In contrast with the heavily urbanized coastal development patterns of the East and West Coasts, Texas developed from the interior out to the coast. With the exception of Galveston, coastal Texas remained largely undeveloped until the 1920s, when the burgeoning oil and gas industry spurred growth. By 1990, fully a third of the population and economic activity in

Texas had located in the coastal zone, even though it contained only a tenth of the state's land area (Texas General Land Office 1990). Nearly 5.5 million residents, 65 percent of the nation's petrochemical industry, and 25 percent of national refining capacity are located on the coast (Culliton et al. 1990).

Texas has experienced the greatest flood and hurricane losses of any state in our study. Between 1978 and 1987, the National Flood Insurance Program paid out over $575 million in flood insurance claims in Texas, constituting about 20 percent of claims paid nationwide (Flood Insurance Producers National Committee 1988). The cause of those losses is not too hard to discern. Approximately 6 percent of Texas is prone to flooding (making it 50 percent above the national average for state flood-prone areas). Texans have not shied away from floodplains as a site for urban development. Over 1 million Texas households live within flood hazard areas, accounting for 11 percent of the national population at risk from flooding (Donnelley Marketing Information Service 1987). With fifteen hurricane landfalls rated as Category 3 or greater between 1899 and 1989, Texas accounted for fully a quarter of the major hurricanes striking U.S. coastlines. Only Florida's twenty-two Category 3 or larger hurricane landfalls amount to more storm activity over this period.

Keeping the State Out of Planning

Living in a politically conservative state with a home rule form of local government, Texans have strong beliefs favoring the free market system, individual property rights, and limited state governmental intervention. Writing on the state's reluctance to participate in the federal coastal zone management program, John DeGrove observed that Texans seem to be "members of a hunting and gathering tribal group whose members view short-term profit making as the key to success, both as individuals and as a society" (cited in Mead 1993, 226). The Texas constitution places numerous limits on state government and diffuses authority through a complex network of semi-autonomous state agencies, special purpose districts, and home rule municipalities. A notable observer of Texas politics maintains that planning goes against Texans' highly individualistic and entrepreneurial cultural values, which are "too focused on maximum exploitation of the environment to give much attention to the problem of how to effectively husband natural resources" (Allen 1989, 3).

Enabling legislation for local planning permits but does not require municipalities to plan and regulate development. In 1989, however, the legislature created a new incentive for local planning. It amended the Local

Government Code to add a section titled "Compliance with Comprehensive Plan," which requires that an adopted comprehensive plan serve as the basis for subsequent amendments to local zoning codes. In other words, local governments can no longer treat their zoning ordinances as if they were plans but instead must adopt a comprehensive land use plan as a separate document. According to Mead (1993), this legislation should lead to a wave of plan making in Texas so that local governments can continue to amend their zoning regulations to accommodate demands for urban development.

Counties in Texas have no authority to plan, and county land use controls are limited to subdivision regulations and public health controls. However, in a landmark piece of legislation (or possibly just an anomaly), the Texas legislature also enacted in 1989 a state mandate that Ellis County prepare a plan, apparently to insure that growth induced by construction of the federally funded superconducting supercollider would be beneficial for the county and the state. That is the first real intrusion of the state in local land use matters and, together with the amendment to the municipal planning legislation noted above, may signal the beginning of a change in how state legislators view local planning matters.

The failure of Texas to adopt a federally recognized coastal management program prior to 1991 also illustrates the state's past reluctance to interfere in local affairs (Curley 1990). In 1974, Texas held a constitutional convention to create a department of natural resources and to establish a coastal zone management program that would qualify for federal funds. This effort failed. Governor Dolph Briscoe then asked the commissioner of the General Land Office, Bob Armstrong, to formulate a coastal management program without express legislative or constitutional authorization. Between 1975 and 1978, Armstrong and a staff of about thirty attempted to craft a program that would emphasize coordination among existing state agencies rather than creation of new regulations or formation of a new coastal management agency. That approach won support in the state legislature, but it was rejected by the federal Office of Coastal Zone Management because the approach lacked specificity and enforceable statewide coastal policies.

The measures demanded by the federal government, however, proved to be unpalatable to the Oil and Gas Association and the Chamber of Commerce, which opposed restrictions on coastal land development and other economic activity, and to local governments, which opposed any limitation of their autonomy. In the fall of 1978, Governor Briscoe (himself a large coastal land owner) removed Armstrong and took on the job of convincing the federal government to accommodate the state's desire for a limited coastal management program (Curley 1990).

In 1978, Republican Bill Clements, a supporter of oil and gas interests, defeated Briscoe on an antigovernment platform. The possibility of federal money was interesting enough that Clements obtained several short-term extensions from the federal Office of Coastal Zone Management in order to evaluate Briscoe's proposed program. The Texas Coastal and Marine Council provided support by passing a resolution in favor of the proposal. Clements named a seven-member task force to modify the draft coastal program, but the legislature refused to provide any funds to regulate state coastal lands.

By the summer of 1979, the program was rechristened the Texas Coastal Program, removing the offending words "zone" and "management." The General Land Office was no longer designated as the oversight agency. Instead, representatives from existing agencies would meet and coordinate existing policies and regulations. The program encompassed all Texas counties bordering the coast. The federal Office of Coastal Zone Management agreed to approve the Texas Coastal Program if the state agreed to fully staff the Texas Energy and Natural Resources Advisory Council and make it the lead agency with the responsibility to coordinate the coastal activities of state agencies into a comprehensive management program.

In October 1980, the Energy and Natural Resources Advisory Council released a draft coastal program for public comment. Oil and gas interests attacked it for curtailing exploration efforts and failing to strike the right balance between public and private interests. Governor Clements remained publicly committed to the program, but he refused to submit it for federal approval. He gave no reasons for this decision, but the executive director of the Energy and Natural Resources Advisory Council at that time said that Clements was heavily influenced by Reagan administration proposals for sharp cutbacks in coastal zone management funding. Thus, the threatened elimination of federal funding effectively killed efforts to get Texas into comprehensive land use management.

By the late 1980s, however, the political climate for coastal management, like that for planning more generally, began to change. In 1989, the legislature designated the General Land Office as lead agency to develop a plan for managing coastal resources. Two years later Governor Ann Richards signed into law the Texas Coastal Management Plan for Beach Access Preservation and Enhancement, Dune Protection, and Coastal Erosion Act. The act requires local government to prepare beach access plans and to designate critical dune areas. This is a limited mandate, but it provides another signal of the Texas legislature's newfound willingness to more aggressively impose state goals and standards on local government.

Single-Purpose Mandates

While resisting comprehensive land use management, the Texas legislature has taken steps to deal in a limited way with various environmental problems, among them the state's vulnerability to natural hazards. Those steps include acts authorizing local flood protection efforts and several coastal laws that provide some hazard mitigation benefits.

Two Texas statutes directly address flood hazards: the Flood Control and Insurance Act and the Water Development Code. Neither mandates participation of local governments. The Flood Control and Insurance Act authorizes local governments to enact regulations that comply with requirements of the National Flood Insurance Program. In many ways, this legislation typifies the traditional Texas response to federal initiatives. The state will comply with federal program requirements if the program offers financial aid and does not lead to reduced state autonomy, require extensive changes in state government, or increase costs.

The principal objective of the Flood Control and Insurance Act is to "procure [insurance coverage] for those citizens of Texas desiring to participate." The National Flood Insurance Program state coordinator for Texas emphasized to us the voluntary nature of the act and noted that legislation that "forces people to comply with big and distant government and interferes with local political autonomy is doomed to failure."

Chapter 51 of the Water Development Code also sets up a voluntary program to foster flood hazard mitigation. Water control and improvement districts are granted the same authority as county governments to tax, issue bonds, and exercise general regulatory powers. Stream and bayou channelization and levees are the most common flood mitigation measures used by the districts. They are typically implemented in a fragmented way, often accomplishing only the transference of storm drainage problems from one jurisdiction to another (Platt 1987).

To deal with fragmentation in water management, chapter 17 of the Water Development Code was enacted in 1985 after a series of costly floods in the early 1980s in the Houston metropolitan area. It authorizes the Texas Water Development Board to make loans for structural and nonstructural flood control measures. Local jurisdictions are eligible for the loans, but each application must represent more than one jurisdiction in order to ensure that flood control projects account for the drainage basin as a whole. As of October 1991, only seven flood control projects had been funded, accounting for $34 million of the $300 million authorized by the state.

Two single-purpose statutes address coastal hazards: the Dune Protection Act and the Coastal Public Lands Management Act. They were enacted in

1973 as part of the unsuccessful effort to participate in the federal coastal zone management program. These statutes are primarily coastal resource protection initiatives, but they also have an impact on natural hazards.

The Dune Protection Act authorizes but does not require county governments to establish a setback zone of up to one thousand feet landward of the Gulf of Mexico shoreline. (Municipalities do not need such authorization because of their home rule powers.) The setback is intended to prevent erosion of natural sand dune systems, which are recognized in the act as the "best natural defense against storms." The act requires minimal land use provisions if counties choose to enact a dune protection line. Only two counties established such lines before June 1990. Staff of the Coastal Division of the Texas General Land Office maintain that county real estate interests consider the lines an unwelcome extension of government bureaucracy that would block commercial development. There was so much concern in the two southernmost coastal counties (Cameron and Willacy) that county officials pressured the legislature to exempt them from the act's grant of authority. In 1991, however, the legislature mandated creation of a dune protection line, and the General Land Office was given rule-making authority in order that state rules take precedence over local ones.

The Coastal Public Lands Management Act authorizes state management and protection of coastal public lands including submerged tidelands, parks, and wildlife refuges. The act includes policy guidelines for setting priorities among alternative land uses and performance standards for assessing the impact of proposed development projects. Coastal storms and shoreline erosion are factors to be considered in making decisions about the use of state property. Policy guidelines for public access, wetland protection, and low development densities have also acted to limit some development in hazard-prone areas.

Finally, we note that unlike the four other states included in this study, Texas does not have a state building code, nor does it require local regulation of building standards. Local governments have sole discretion to enact (or refrain from enacting) construction standards to prevent losses from high, hurricane-driven winds or to require that structures be elevated above base flood elevations.

Washington: Strong Single-Purpose Mandates

Population growth in Washington accelerated after the 1962 Seattle World's Fair brought national attention to the Puget Sound region. With much of that growth concentrated in areas of western Washington that are exposed to flood, seismic, and volcanic hazards, the public's exposure to natural hazards has increased as well. This growing risk has attracted some attention from state policy makers, but prior to 1990 Washington steered clear of coordinated state growth management.

Flood risk in Washington is the lowest of the five states studied, but it is still substantial. More than ninety thousand households and $3 billion in property are at risk from a hundred-year-flood event (Donnelley Marketing Information Service 1987). Past earthquakes include a 1949 event near Olympia registering 7.1 on the Richter scale and a 1965 event between Seattle and Tacoma registering 6.5 on the Richter scale. The Olympia earthquake caused eight deaths and nearly $150 million in damages, and the Seattle-Tacoma earthquake caused seven deaths and nearly $50 million in damages (in 1984 dollars). However, much larger events could occur. Recent research indicates a subduction-type earthquake of Richter magnitude 8.0 or greater is possible along the coastal margin of Oregon and Washington, causing longer periods of ground shaking and affecting a broader geographic area than previously thought likely (Nosson, Quamar, and Thorsen 1988).

The eruption of Mount St. Helens on May 18, 1980, illustrates the volcanic hazard. This event, triggered by a magnitude 5.1 earthquake beneath the volcano, spewed as much as five inches of ash over an area of twenty thousand square miles and seriously disrupted activity in numerous communities. Including the effects of the lateral blast, debris avalanche, mud flows, flooding, and ash fallout, the eruption resulted in approximately $1.1 billion in losses (Tilling 1987).

Keeping the State Out of Planning

As in Texas, governing authority in Washington is diffused through an extensive network of elected commissions, home rule cities, and diverse special districts. Before 1990, the state deferred to local governments in land use and building matters. One commentator described Washington as having perhaps "the nation's most confusing pattern of constitutional and statutory authority for local land-use planning and regulation" (Settle 1983, 4).

The 1935 planning-enabling legislation permitted but did not require cities and counties to plan and regulate land use. Increased growth in unincorporated areas led to the enactment of the County Planning Enabling Act of 1963 and the Optional Municipal Code of 1967. Neither of these statutes required planning. Instead, they specified requirements if counties or code-designated cities chose to plan. Neither specifically addressed natural hazards.

Although state policy makers eschewed comprehensive growth management until the 1990s, calls for state intervention to manage growth date back to the early 1960s. In the face of increasing urbanization in western Washington, a Citizens' Advisory Committee submitted a report to the Joint Legislative Committee on Urban Growth calling for curbs on urban sprawl, acquisition of parks and open space, a balanced transportation system with a strong emphasis on mass transit, and a comprehensive state land use and facilities plan. However, no legislation was forthcoming.

In 1971, the legislature formed the Washington State Land Planning Commission to review land-planning policies and to draft new planning legislation for the 1973 session. Bills were introduced based on the recommendations of the commission, but they also were rejected. The report summarized the status of land use planning in the state as follows:

> Most regulation of land use today is done under enabling laws passed 35 years ago. But times have changed, and the laws which seemed inadequate in the past are now totally inadequate . . . innovative planning by local governments is often restricted by state law. The existing statutes do not require land-use plans to be specific enough for results to be measured and evaluated, and the plans are frequently allowed to become obsolete. Furthermore, state guidance is lacking or inadequate in most cases and a comprehensive state policy is nonexistent. (Washington State Land Planning Commission 1973)

State growth management came up again in 1978, when Governor Dixie Lee Ray appointed a Working Group on Growth Management comprised of senior staff members of nine state agencies with an interest in growth patterns in the state. The group identified several areas of concern that included the need for local authority to manage growth. No comprehensive growth management legislation was proposed.

By 1990, however, rapid population increases in the Puget Sound region created citizen demands for more-effective management of growth. The state legislature responded with new growth management legislation in 1990 (House Bill 2929), which was strengthened through amendments passed in 1991 (see DeGrove 1992 and Smith 1993 for detailed descriptions of the program). This new planning legislation borrows heavily from the growth management laws in Oregon and Florida and includes a system to assure the siting of essential public facilities. The Washington act includes some strong provisions, such as required state agency compliance with mandated local comprehensive plans, a set of growth management hearing boards to assure that local plans are consistent with state goals, and procedures to assure the conservation of agricultural, forest, and mineral lands and critical areas. While only Washington's faster-growing counties (and cities within them) are required to comply with the comprehensive-planning provisions, all cities and counties must adopt development regulations to protect natural resources and critical areas.

A review of the program by planning educator Gary Pivo (1993) found that most of the affected local governments were making progress in meeting the basic goals of the legislation but at a slower pace than originally envisioned and with more variation in effort than desired. Pivo criticized the growth management legislation passed in 1990 and 1991 for giving too much discretion to local decision makers and providing too little state oversight of local planning matters.

Single-Purpose Mandates

In contrast with Texas, which has generally steered clear of state interference in local government land use management, the Washington legislature long ago adopted a number of single-purpose measures that affect local land use decisions. These include (1) a law, similar to California's environmental quality act, that requires consideration of environmental impacts in the issuing of permits for land development; (2) a state role in regulating building to achieve seismic safety objectives; (3) regulation of shoreline development through state-mandated local shoreline management and permit issuance; and (4) state standards for flood hazard mitigation.

Washington enacted the State Environmental Policy Act (SEPA) in 1971 as part of a comprehensive package of environmental legislation proposed by Governor Dan Evans. It raised little controversy and was signed into law without public comment. The act requires state and local governments to review the environmental consequences of proposed projects that include development proposed by the private sector.

Challenges to SEPA have been based on the vagueness of the statutory language, the review criteria, and the scope of its coverage (Settle 1983). The building and real estate industry succeeded in convincing the 1981 legislature to consider watering SEPA down, but the amendments were vetoed by Governor John Spellman. Spellman appointed a bipartisan review committee to develop amendments that would clarify the situations in which an environmental impact statement would be required, lessen the administrative burdens faced by large developers, and improve the quality of environmental decision making. The committee's proposed amendments also permitted cities and counties to designate environmentally sensitive areas, which are defined by statute to include areas with unstable soils, steep slopes, unusual flora and fauna, wetlands, and floodplains. Normally exempt activities would be subject to SEPA review if located within a designated environmentally sensitive area. These amendments were enacted in 1983 and 1984.

The original state building code, motivated by the 1949 Olympia earthquake, required hospitals, schools, places of public assembly, and publicly owned structures in western Washington to be built to resist specified earthquake intensities. This legislation was not widely implemented, and the specified intensities were woefully deficient. In separate actions in the 1950s and 1960s, about 80 percent of larger Washington cities adopted building codes with seismic provisions. Following the Seattle-Tacoma earthquake of 1965 and the 1971 San Fernando earthquake in southern California, seismic provisions were included in a mandatory state building code enacted in 1975. This legislation established a new state building code based on the Uniform Building Code; it mandated local compliance with the code and created mechanisms for updating code provisions and for monitoring local compliance (Washington State Building Code Council 1989).

Shoreline erosion and coastal flood hazards are addressed by the Shoreline Management Act. This act directs the state to prepare guidelines for shoreline land uses and requires local governments to prepare shoreline master programs consistent with state guidelines for land within two hundred feet of the Pacific Ocean, Puget Sound, the Straits of San Juan DeFuca, and other bodies of water. The legislation directs local government to regulate land use within the shoreline protection area. The state may adopt regulations if local governments fail to act. The state is also authorized to directly regulate such land uses as power plants that are deemed to be of statewide significance. The guidelines for local programs promote flood hazard management consistent with state floodplain management legislation.

In 1935, in response to a series of severe floods, Washington enacted a floodplain management statute. The legislation required the state to designate flood control zones and regulate floodplain land use through state flood control zone permits. As in California, which has similar legislation, state floodplain management efforts were superseded by enactment in 1968 of the National Flood Insurance Program (NFIP).

Over time the state role grew under the federal program, and by 1987 the state of Washington had enacted floodplain management provisions, administered by the Department of Ecology, that are stronger than the federal NFIP provisions (Washington Department of Ecology 1988). In addition, through the Flood Control Assistance Account Program, adopted by the legislature in 1984, state planners in the department have an important incentive they can use to stimulate local government interest in resolving flood problems. The program provides funds, on a matching basis, for the preparation of floodplain management plans and for various flood control works. Since its passage, the state has provided $4 million per biennium in grants to local governments (Louthain 1994).

Concluding Note

After 1990 both Texas and Washington took steps to strengthen the state role in development management. Texas finally put together a coastal management program that met with federal approval, and Washington adopted a state growth management law that establishes stringent standards for planning and growth management for fast-growing counties. Those efforts moved Texas into the mainstream and Washington into a leadership position in state comprehensive planning.

Although both states, to different degrees, have come to recognize some of the benefits of planning, they differ in important respects. A recent article about planning in Texas is titled, "This Is Texas, Not California or Florida" (Mead 1993). The author emphasizes the fact that, like the majority of states, Texas has not rushed to deal with problems of growth by enacting a state plan or centralizing planning and regulatory powers at the state level. Instead, in keeping with the laissez-faire political culture dominant there, it prefers to vest control over land use issues in local governments. In this regard, it is similar to how the state of North Carolina has dealt with growth issues in the western, mountain part of the state.

In contrast, Washington has a long history of state intervention through single-purpose mandates to accomplish various environmental protection and hazard mitigation goals. The 1990 growth management legislation, which went into effect after the field data collection for this book, merely extends that tradition to include systematic land use planning for entire jurisdictions. As we will see in a later chapter, most Washington jurisdictions already had land use plans, so the new law was not as revolutionary in nature as it seems on its face. For our purposes, the key opportunity we gain by studying Washington prior to the 1990 law is the opportunity to compare this state and its strong single-purpose mandates with other states that added comprehensive-planning mandates to the single-purpose approach. Texas and the North Carolina mountains then stand as the cases of base, minimal state intervention.

II

Mandate Design and Outcomes

6

Designing and Implementing Mandates

The depiction of the evolution of state mandates underscores the variety of approaches taken by states to make local governments plan and manage development. Perhaps what we observe is little more than a series of idiosyncratic decisions being played out in state capitols, city halls, and planning departments. However, we think there is much more to it than state and local policy making by the seat of the pants. We suggest that there are several sets of factors that structure as well as ease local planning and development management. Of interest in this chapter is how different provisions of state mandates influence actions undertaken by relevant state agencies as they go about the business of carrying out the policies. Evidence of a strong linkage between mandate intent, as specified in the design of the policy, and actions undertaken by relevant state agencies is required for concluding that state mandates are effective.

Regardless of whether one is considering comprehensive-planning or single-purpose mandates, the design of a policy mandate is potentially important in shaping agency actions. The state policies we consider differ markedly with respect to key provisions. One set of differences concerns the policy prescriptions contained in planning and single-purpose mandates. A second set of differences lies with the extent to which they incorporate various inducements, system changes, or capacity-building features that might ease intergovernmental implementation. This chapter examines the ways in which these different features shape implementation.

Civics books teach us that state agencies are the administrative arms of legislatures. However, a good deal of research on public bureaucracies shows that government agencies take additional cues from other sources. Conflicting demands arise from legislative sources, program beneficiaries, and other interests that are affected by the policy. Limited resources make it impossible for agencies to give high priority to all of the tasks they are asked to undertake. These problems are more acute when mandates do not adequately signal intent, guide agency actions, or provide sufficient incentives or other inducements for agencies to carry out necessary actions. Because comprehensive-planning mandates are by their nature more complex and less directed than single-purpose mandates, planning mandates are particularly prone to distortions in policy implementation. An important aspect of this chapter's examination of the translation of policy into practice is its assessment of the extent to which comprehensive-planning mandates suffer from these limitations.

Two aspects of policy implementation serve as focal points for the analyses of this chapter. One is the implementation style adopted by relevant state agencies in their dealings with local governments: Do they adopt a cooperative stance toward local governments that emphasizes compliance with the spirit, but not necessarily the letter, of the mandate? Or do they seek strict compliance with the provisions of mandate? This is important to understand because comprehensive-planning mandates tend to emphasize intergovernmental collaboration, and such collaboration may be seriously undermined if facilitative approaches are not adopted by relevant state agencies. Yet bringing about such collaboration is not likely to be easy. The second aspect of policy implementation that is relevant is the degree of effort that state agencies put into implementation. This is important in establishing the seriousness with which state mandates are pursued.

Our examination of the differences in policy design among states and between comprehensive-planning and single-purpose mandates sets the stage for thinking about implementation challenges and prospects. In discussing these, we first turn to consideration of the differences in implementation style adopted by state agencies when carrying out either form of policy mandate. We ask how that style is influenced by the features of mandates and other forces. We next consider the variation in degree of effort among relevant state agencies, asking the parallel questions of how effort is influenced by the features of mandates and other forces. These two sets of analyses lead us to draw conclusions about the translation of policy into practice at the state level.

Design of State Mandates

The design of state mandates governing land use and development actions can be examined in a variety of ways. Commentators about such policies typically address the substantive features, such as the planning and consistency requirements of growth management programs we considered in chapter 1. However, the appropriate foci with respect to implementation prospects are the policy features that either ease or hinder the ability of state agencies to carry out the policies. In considering various attributes of the design of state mandates, our interest here is in how policy design helps structure implementation. Throughout the chapter we consider attributes that previous research (for overviews see Goggin et al. 1990; Mazmanian and Sabatier 1983) has suggested are important in these regards.

One aspect of policy design is the complexity of the policy, which relates to the range and consistency of policy objectives. The presumption from prior research is that statutory coherence brought about by clear goals and simpler implementation structures will enhance prospects for smooth implementation. Complex implementation structures and indirect control brought about by multiple actors, decision points, and levels of action can undermine implementation. Critics of this statutory coherence tenet argue that prescriptions for clear goals and simple implementation structures do not reflect the inherently complex linkages among agencies and levels of government or the need for goals to be written vaguely in order to attract enough support to enact policies.

A second design feature is the set of provisions aimed at facilitating implementation, which we label as commitment- and capacity-building features. These are policy provisions directing state agencies to build commitment of local governments to the goals of the legislation or to build their capacity to accomplish specified objectives. Specifying the tools for building capacity or commitment within legislation sets expectations for state agencies as they carry out the policy. The presumption is that as the expectations become more extensive, state agencies find it more difficult to ignore the mandate and as a consequence expend more effort in carrying out the policy.

A third feature consists of the persuasive tools that state agencies are authorized or required to use in seeking compliance with state objectives by local governments. As noted in the introductory chapter, states rely to varying degrees on two sets of tools to persuade local governments to prepare plans or otherwise carry out state wishes. Coercion is one tool. It involves monitoring local actions and applying sanctions for those that do not meet program requirements. Incentives are a second set of tools. Typical incentives include provision of financial and technical assistance.

Note that state mandates also typically specify penalties and other coercive features that relate to the failure of the private sector to adhere to various requirements. These are usually imposed by local governments acting as agents of state government. These can be distinguished from the mandate features that relate to requirements that local governments produce plans or carry out other actions.

Differences among States

One way of characterizing the design of state planning mandates is to consider key attributes of the policies. Figure 6.1 compares key attributes for the planning mandates in California, Florida, and North Carolina. For each state, the figure shows ratings of the complexity of policy design, the extent to which mandates authorize the use of coercion in seeking compliance by local governments, and the amount of effort expended by state agencies in implementing the policies. Not shown are comparisons of the degree to which the policies incorporate facilitating tools and the differences in styles among state agencies when dealing with local governments.

Based on the policy design scores, California can be characterized as having a weak comprehensive-planning mandate. Relative to other states with planning mandates, California is more permissive. This is reflected by very limited provisions for sanctioning local governments that fail to comply with planning requirements. The emphasis is on prescribing the elements of plans rather than ensuring compliance with a planning process. California is also notable for having the lowest score for effort that state agencies put into carrying out the comprehensive-planning mandate.

Florida presents a very different case in that it has, relative to the other states, a strong planning mandate. Florida combines coercive provisions (for dealing with local governments that fail to comply with planning requirements) and provisions for building the capacity of local governments to undertake planning. Florida has the highest score for the effort that state agencies put into carrying out the planning mandate.

North Carolina's moderate planning requirements fall between those of California and Florida. The mandate, which applies only to the North Carolina coastal region, is less complex in design than Florida's and California's planning mandates. The North Carolina policy has some of the coercive and capacity-building attributes found in the Florida planning mandate. The key

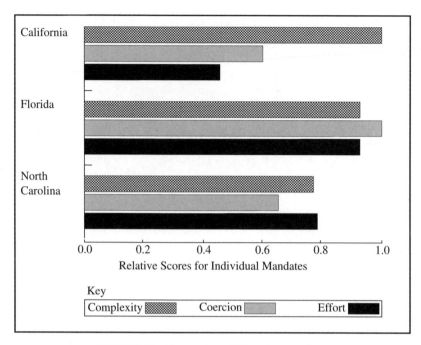

FIGURE 6.1 Comparison of Planning Mandates
NOTE: The measures of the different attributes are discussed in the methodological appendix. For comparative purposes each of the measures has been converted to a scale of zero to one.

difference is that North Carolina places more emphasis than California on legal formalism in dealings with local governments. Like Florida, North Carolina scores relatively high in terms of effort devoted to implementing the planning mandate.

It is also useful to depict the differences among states with respect to single-purpose mandates. California can be characterized as having strong environmental regulation on paper. As with the planning requirements, the state devotes relatively little effort to carrying out the single-purpose policies. Florida presents a very different case entailing a strong set of single-purpose mandates backed by strong effort by state agencies to carry them out. As with the planning mandate, North Carolina's single-purpose mandates fall between those of California and Florida. North Carolina's two single-purpose mandates rate among the least coercive and prescriptive, accompanied by an average level of effort devoted by state agencies to carrying them out.

Texas, at the time of our study, had two single-purpose mandates for addressing hazards. The two mandates can be characterized as constituting minimalist intervention in local government or private affairs. In comparison with the other single-purpose mandates, those in Texas are more permissive in that they encourage, rather than demand, action by local governments. This is reflected in lower mandate coercion scores, moderate provisions for building the capacity of local governments, and a more conciliatory agency implementation style. The limited agency implementation effort is also reflective of a minimalist approach.

Washington's bundle of four single-purpose mandates provides a stark contrast to the single-purpose mandates in Texas in that Washington's policy makers have set forth focused policies for managing different aspects of the environment. Relative to other single-purpose mandates, the policies of Washington state rank third in coercive features and second in terms of implementation efforts by state agencies. The relatively strong state effort to carry out these policies is backed by legal formalism in state agency dealings with local governments.

Differences in Types of Mandate

Another way of comparing design features of mandates is to consider differences between the policy design of comprehensive-planning and single-purpose mandates while recognizing that there is variation within each type. These comparisons are shown in figure 6.2, which shows the mean scores for each type of policy mandate with respect to various attributes of policy design and implementation.

The most obvious differences are with respect to the complexity of mandates and the clarity of mandate goals. At least on paper, comprehensive-planning mandates look messy in comparison with most single-purpose mandates. The planning policies entail multiple and often vague goals, assignment of responsibility to multiple agencies at different levels of government, and complex administrative structures. Complexity and lack of goal clarity may be a nemesis for successful implementation. However, comprehensive-planning mandates, in theory at least, provide the means for adapting mandate prescriptions to meet local circumstances. In contrast, single-purpose mandates provide a more rigid approach in prescribing local governmental actions and desired private sector behaviors.

Other than the complexity of the policies and their lack of goal clarity, the distinction between various attributes for the two types of mandates is more a matter of degree than of sharp contrasts. Nonetheless, differences in the average ratings for design attributes for the two types of mandates evidence

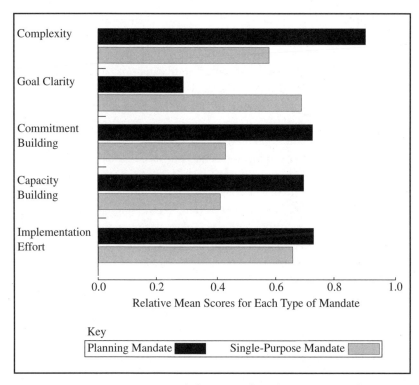

FIGURE 6.2 Comparison of Planning and Single-Purpose Mandates

NOTE: The measures of the different attributes are discussed in the methodological appendix. For comparative purposes each of the measures has been converted to a scale of zero to one. The scores for the bundle of single-purpose mandates in each state consist of a weighted average of scores for the relevant mandates for a given state. Weights were assigned according to the relative importance of each mandate in addressing natural hazards. No aggregation or weighting was required for comprehensive-planning mandates, since there is only one planning mandate for each of the relevant states.

subtle distinctions (some of which are not shown in figure 6.2). The adaptive aspects of planning mandates are reflected in the greater extent to which they authorize measures to build the commitment of local governments to state goals and the capacity of local governments to carry out policies.

The two types of mandates differ little in terms of implementation effort expended by state agencies and the style of state agencies in their dealings with local governments. Here again the distinction is a matter of degree more than of contrast. Some argue that comprehensive-planning mandates have an advantage of combining agency energies across a number of goals. We find, however, that implementation effort is at best only slightly greater on average for comprehensive-planning mandates than for single-purpose mandates. Reflecting their more collaborative nature, the approach that state agencies take in dealing with local governments when carrying out planning mandates is somewhat more accommodating on average than it is for single-purpose mandates.

In sum, the real differences from an implementation perspective between comprehensive-planning and single-purpose mandates are the added complexity of the planning mandates and their commensurate decrease in clarity of policy objectives. These are not trivial differences, since complexity and vague goals have been shown by implementation scholars to be stumbling blocks to effective implementation. Yet others argue that such problems can be overcome through inclusion within policies of an appropriate mix of facilitating features to help ease implementation difficulties. In the remainder of the chapter, we provide an assessment of the role of various mandate features in shaping the implementation styles and the level of effort of state agencies charged with carrying out the policies under study. This provides a basis for assessing the extent to which the complexity of planning mandates acts to undermine their implementation.

Shaping State Agency Approaches to Local Governments

The day-to-day realities of mandates are manifested by state agency dealings with local governments, particularly in situations where local governments are unwilling to follow the procedures that mandates prescribe. Legislative mandates and executive orders provide directives for state agency action, but the signals contained in those directives are sometimes muddled or inconsistent. Of interest is the way in which state agencies interpret such signals in their day-to-day dealings with local governments: Do state officials seek strict compliance by local governments with mandate provisions? Or do state officials negotiate compliance with local governments?

The approach of state agencies in dealing with local governments, what we call implementation style, is particularly important to consider for state planning mandates. The collaborative state and local relationship that is called for in planning mandates would be undermined if state agencies followed a by-the-book approach to their dealings with local governments. But bringing about the desired collaboration is not easy, especially when the state and local partners have a history of mistrust and differences over policy objectives. Policies must be designed to provide incentives for cooperation, and state agencies responsible for implementing the policies must reflect that philosophy in their day-to-day dealings with local governments.

In order to understand the role of mandates in shaping the implementation styles of state agencies, we consider variation in implementation styles for each of the three comprehensive-planning mandates and fifteen of the sixteen single-purpose mandates for the five states in our study. (Data were unavailable for rating the style used in implementing the Florida state building code.) The individual mandates provide a sufficient number of cases to statistically assess the role of different factors in shaping the implementation styles that agencies have employed. Stated differently, for these analyses and the remainder of this chapter, we shift from looking at states and different types of mandates to analyzing variation in the way in which individual mandates are carried out by state agencies.

Variation in Approach of State Agencies

Following Gormley (1989; also see Gruber 1987), we conceptualize the implementation style of state agencies as a continuum running from an informal, flexible approach in negotiating compliance to a formal, legalistic approach in dealing with local governments. From our surveys of state agencies, we were able to create an index of implementation style.[1] (The details are provided in the methodological appendix.) Table 6.1 shows the ranking of the various mandates in terms of implementation style with the more formal, legalistic approaches at the top and the more informal, flexible approaches at the bottom of the table. The median score of 4.20 (out of a possible 7.0) reflects a somewhat coercive approach in dealing with local governments. More than one-third of the agencies use this more formal, legalistic style of implementation.

A sense of the differences in style in state agency dealings with local governments is evident from the comments respondents made about agency implementation approaches. One Florida respondent, remarking on the more formal, legalistic approach in implementing coastal and beach provisions, noted that the agency used sanctions without hesitation and employed

---

1. Implementation style is conceptually distinct from the degree of effort agencies expend in carrying out policies, since mandate provisions can in principle be implemented with a range of styles. For the eighteen mandates under study, the Pearson correlation between implementation style and implementation effort (when transformed by a logarithmic function for statistical reasons) is $-.23$. That is, a more formal and legalistic style is associated with less effort.

TABLE 6.1

Ranking of Implementation Styles of State Agencies

Legislation Governing Agency Actions	Rating[a]
California state building code	6.80
California flood hazard requirements	6.00
California earthquake mandates	5.33
Washington State Environmental Protection Act	5.33
Florida Beach and Shore Preservation Act	5.10
Washington Shoreline Management Act	5.00
Washington State Floodplain Management Act	4.80
North Carolina Coastal Area Management Act[b]	4.50
California Planning Act[b]	4.33
North Carolina flood hazard executive orders	4.20
Florida Environmental Land and Water Management Act	3.78
Washington state building code	3.67
California Environmental Quality Act	3.50
Texas Dune Protection and Coastal Management Acts	3.40
California Coastal Act	3.40
Texas Flood Control and Insurance Act	3.40
Florida Local Government Comprehensive Planning and Land Development Act[b]	3.00
North Carolina state building code	2.00

[a] Index of state agency approach to local governments, as rated by survey respondents. Higher scores indicate more formal, legalistic approaches; lower scores indicate more informal, flexible approaches. Data for rating the Florida building code are unavailable.
[b] Comprehensive-planning mandate.

extensive documentation for potential litigation. Staff limitations forced the agency to be oriented toward process more than outcome. The other end of the continuum is reflected in comments concerning Florida's comprehensive-planning mandate. One respondent from the relevant state agency noted that sanctions regarding plan compliance were talked about more than actually imposed. Indeed, only 5 of 457 local governments received sanctions for failing to meet state deadlines for preparing a plan. The agency used an accommodating approach as much as possible by negotiating compliance agreements as a means of avoiding legal battles in the courts.

A more mixed approach is evident from the comments of one respondent involved in the state of Washington's floodplain management program: "Depending on the local situation, we consult or take more aggressive enforcement action; we want flood reduction any way we can get it." A similar mixed picture is provided by a respondent involved in implementing Florida's Environmental Land and Water Management Act in noting that the agency chooses battles for enforcement. If the development is of little precedent and entails relatively low stakes, then the agency negotiates, saving litigation for large matters that set precedent.

The Role of State Mandates in Shaping Implementation Style

Can the legislative provisions that constitute a mandate affect the behavior of state agencies in dealing with local governments? According to implementation scholars (see, e.g., Goggin et al. 1990; Van Meter and Van Horn 1975), one of the key functions of policy design (i.e., legislative provisions) is to establish signals about expectations for different agencies. Applying this general notion to the mandates under study suggests that differing mixes of persuasive provisions within state mandates establish different messages about the approach state agencies are expected to employ when dealing with local governments. Mandates that authorize the use of coercion signal that agencies are to use a "get tough" approach. Mandates that authorize the use of incentives signal a more accommodating approach. These signals are likely to be clearer when the policy design is less complex and goals are clearly articulated. However, the signaling is likely to be imperfect, since it is tempered by the degree of commitment that state agencies have to the policy goals and their capacity for carrying out the policies.

In order to understand the factors that shape agency implementation style, we developed a statistical model for the approaches that state agencies employed for the eighteen mandates under study. The primary explanatory factors of interest are two attributes of the design of mandates that provide signals about implementation style: the means that state agencies are authorized to employ to persuade local governments to comply with procedural requirements (i.e., the mix of incentives and coercion) and the complexity of mandate design (measured by an index of goal clarity). In order to capture the potential influence of a host of situational factors that affect the influence of mandate legislation on agency behavior, our statistical models include measures of the commitment of state agencies to policy goals and their capacity to carry out the policies.

The statistical results suggest that the mix of persuasive means is important in shaping implementation styles.[2] In particular, the adoption of more-formal, legalistic approaches by state agencies is associated with mandates

2. The statistical analysis involved an ordinary least squares regression, correcting for heteroskedasticity using procedures contained in the Systat statistical package. The adjusted coefficient of determination is .22 ($F = 2.49$; $N = 18$). Alternative corrections for heteroskedasticity using weighted least squares estimation provided a statistically signifi-

that authorize the use of coercion in seeking compliance by local governments. Yet an equally strong influence is the mediating effect of agency commitment and capacity. As explained below, our modeling shows that the direction of influence of persuasive measures authorized in mandate legislation is contingent upon the level of commitment and capacity of implementing agencies. The statistical modeling also suggests (but with less certainty) that increased clarity of goals makes it easier for state agencies to employ formal, legalistic approaches to dealing with local governments.

One of the key findings from this analysis is the influence of the mix of persuasive measures upon the style of implementation. Authorizations in mandates for state agencies to use coercion when dealing with local governments has a greater effect on agency implementation style than we anticipated. Our modeling shows that increasing coercive provisions from those of the median set of provisions among the mandates studied to those of the seventy-fifth percentile results in an increase in the degree of formalism from the median of all mandates to nearly the eightieth percentile in legal formalism. As the balance of coercive versus incentive measures increases, the "get tough" signal of the legislation becomes clearer and leads to increased pressures for agencies to employ a more legal and formalistic style in dealing with local governments. The presence of coercive provisions enhances the legal authority and means with which agencies can take formal actions. As the balance tilts toward incentives and away from coercion, the signal is to adopt a more accommodating approach in dealing with local governments.

While these signals are important, our results also suggest that they are far from perfect. Simply mandating a "get tough" approach does not ensure that agencies will follow through. In this regard, Bardach and Kagan (1982; also see Hedge, Menzel, and Williams 1988) argue that the attitude toward a given set of policy directives on the part of those charged with carrying them out acts as an important mediating factor in the way in which the directive is pursued. As noted by William Gormley (1992), state agencies might be reluctant coercive agents, may not fully understand what is required of them, or may not possess the resources to carry out enforcement tasks. Similarly, sending out signals that cooperation is desired may be insufficient if agency personnel have previously adopted legalistic approaches or if agency personnel do not have the expertise to negotiate compliance.

---

cant model ($F = 4.56, p < .05$) but created more difficulty for conveying results. The standardized regression coefficient for mandate coercion is .42 ($p < .05$), for goal clarity is .33 ($p > .05$), and for an interaction of agency commitment and capacity is $-.50$ ($p < .05$).

The influence of the clarity of policy goals (and less complex implementation structures) on legal formalism is less noteworthy than other factors in our statistical modeling (see note 2). The overall pattern across a number of statistical models indicates that clear goals make it easier for agencies to use a more formal, legalistic style in dealing with local governments. Those who write about legal formalism in regulation underscore the importance of clear provisions as a basis for enforcement and litigation (e.g., Bardach and Kagan 1982). Our findings of a somewhat weak influence reflects a different dynamic, which is also reflected in the organizational literature (e.g., Wilson 1989, 158-71). This literature suggests that organizations resort to legalistic interpretations when goals are confusing and tasks are complicated, particularly when it is difficult to assess the outcome of agency actions.

The most noteworthy finding from our statistical modeling (note 2) concerns the influence of state agency commitment and capacity on implementation style. These factors alone account for some 12 percent of the variation in implementation styles. The influence of these two factors also reflects organizational dynamics. As agencies increase their commitment to the goals sought by mandates and their capacity for achieving the goals, two things happen. First, the agencies are more willing to support achievement of the goals. Second, they are more able to deal with local governments in a cooperative, flexible manner. Limited commitment leads to token efforts to implement programs, achieved through quick and easy enforcement by following letter-of-the-law, legalistic approaches. Limited capacity reduces the ability of agencies to negotiate or undertake other flexible actions, which requires ample staff resources and time.

Our modeling of the effects of agency commitment and capacity shows that the influence of these factors is not straightforward. We undertook additional statistical modeling to sort out the influence of different combinations of levels of agency commitment and capacity (see May 1993). These analyses suggest that when agency commitment and capacity are both strong, the combined effect facilitates an informal, flexible style of implementation. When commitment is strong and capacity weak, the combined effect stimulates a more formal, legalistic style. For the other two combinations, the effect is negligible.

Stated differently, the level of commitment of state agencies to the goals of mandates and their capacity for carrying out the policies act as noteworthy factors in shaping agency implementation style. Both commitment and capacity need to be strong for agencies to adopt an accommodating style of implementation. This is because higher agency commitment and capacity provide greater freedom and confidence in pursuing more cooperative approaches. If capacity is weak, increased agency commitment only adds to legal formalism. When agencies have low levels of capacity for implementing the objectives of a mandate, there is insufficient slack to respond to increased pressure to adopt conciliatory approaches. The coping response to increased commitment, absent requisite capacity, is to adopt a style that is process oriented and formal.

Enhancing Agency Efforts to Implement Policies

State agencies often must make hard choices among the multiple mandates they are charged with implementing. In setting priorities among important mandates, agency officials at least implicitly consider the difficulty of the tasks, the availability of resources, and the ramifications of playing down a given mandate or elements of a mandate. Given these pressures, it would seem that the mix of provisions in a mandate would have little influence in enhancing the efforts of relevant state agencies to carry out planning or single-purpose policies. Yet it would also seem that the specification of different policy features would be important in setting expectations for state agencies. These expectations, in turn, provide important signals as to how seriously policy makers take particular mandates.

In order to understand the role of mandates in enhancing the efforts of state agencies to carry out policies, we discuss a parallel set of analyses to those undertaken for understanding variation in the implementation styles of state agencies. In this section, we consider variation in the effort that is expended by state agencies in implementing each of the three comprehensive-planning mandates and the sixteen single-purpose mandates.

Variation in Implementation Effort of State Agencies

We think of implementation effort as a discount factor applied to the intentions of state legislators. Strong efforts by relevant state agencies to carry out a policy, comprised of many resources devoted to a program and extensive activities, entail little discounting of the goals of legislation. Weak agency implementation efforts entail substantial discounting. As discussed in the methodological appendix, we characterize implementation effort of state agencies in terms of an index based on expenditures for the hazards components of each mandate. To make these data more comparable, we report state expenditures divided by the number of jurisdictions affected by a given mandate.

TABLE 6.2

Ranking of Implementation Efforts of State Agencies

Legislation Governing Agency Actions	Effort[a]
California Coastal Act	$64,500
Florida Beach and Shore Preservation Act	34,000
Florida Local Government Comprehensive Planning and Land Development Act[b]	28,500
Florida Environmental Land and Water Management Act	23,600
Washington State Floodplain Management Act	7,500
North Carolina Coastal Area Management Act[b]	6,500
North Carolina state building code	2,500
California flood hazard requirements	1,900
California earthquake mandates	1,800
Washington Shoreline Management Act	1,500
Florida State Minimum Building Code	1,100
Washington State Building Code	700
Washington State Environmental Protection Act	600
North Carolina flood hazard executive orders	500
Texas Dune Protection and Coastal Management Acts	300
Texas Flood Control and Insurance Act	300
California Planning Act[b]	200
California Environmental Quality Act	100
California state building code	100

[a] Expenditure per affected jurisdiction on hazards component of the mandate (rounded), 1990–91.

[b] Comprehensive-planning mandate.

Table 6.2 shows a ranking of the effort, measured in terms of financial expenditure, that state agencies devote to the different mandates. The mandates with strong implementation efforts (those in the upper quartile) had a median 1990 expenditure of $28,500 for each local government affected by the mandate. In contrast, the mandates with weak implementation efforts (those in the lower quartile) had a median expenditure of $200 in 1990 expenditures per affected jurisdiction.

The mandates that affect large numbers of jurisdictions tend to have weaker implementation efforts than those mandates affecting fewer jurisdictions. Yet this is not uniformly the case. Florida's planning mandate affects nearly as many jurisdictions as any of California's mandates. But the effort devoted by state agencies in Florida to implementing the planning mandate is more than one hundred times that of the corresponding effort made by California agencies for its planning act, environmental quality program, or state building code (the latter shown at the bottom of table 6.2).

The Role of State Mandates in Increasing Implementation Effort

Can the provisions of mandates influence the effort that state agencies expend on a given mandate? In order to assess the influence of mandate design and other factors on implementation effort, we developed a statistical model explaining variation in effort for nineteen mandates. For this model, the primary explanatory factors of interest are the attributes of the legislation creating the mandate that signal policy import: the extent to which facilitating features are authorized by the legislation, the specification of means to persuade local governments to comply, and the clarity of policy goals written into the law. We also include measures of the commitment of state agencies to the goals of the mandates and the capacity of state agencies to carry out the policies. The construction of the measures is discussed in the methodological appendix.

The statistical results suggest that the number of facilitating features (i.e., provisions directing state agencies to build the commitment of local governments to the goals of the legislation or to build their capacity to accomplish specified objectives) and the extent of agency commitment are strong influences on the degree of effort that agencies devote to a given mandate.[3] Increased authority to use coercion in dealing with local governments (e.g., in withholding revenue payments) also acts to enhance implementation effort, but this effect is weaker than the influence of other aspects of the design of mandates. One unexpected finding is the failure to conclude that differences in the clarity of goals or differences in agency capacity influence implementation effort. The factors we analyze account for 44 percent of the variation in the implementation efforts of state agencies.

The most noteworthy finding concerns the large influence on implementation effort of changes in the extent to which commitment- or capacity-building provisions are specified as part of a mandate. If the extent of either of the two facilitating features is increased from the median value of all man-

---

3. The statistical analysis involved an ordinary least squares regression, correcting for heteroskedasticity using procedures contained in the Systat statistical package. The adjusted coefficient of determination is .44 ($F = 3.79$, $p < .01$, $N = 19$). The standardized regression coefficient for mandate facilitating features is .68 ($p < .01$), for mandate coercion is .29 ($p > .05$), for goal clarity is .01 ($p > .05$), for agency capacity is $-.07$ ($p > .05$), and for agency commitment is .45 ($p < .05$). A logarithmic transformation was applied to the dependent variable in order to meet the regression assumption of linearity.

dates to that of the seventy-fifth percentile, we project a 6 to 8 percent increase in implementation effort.[4] If the extent of both features has a corresponding increase, then we project a 19 percent increase in implementation effort.

Several things are involved in directing state agencies to build the commitment and capacity of local governments. Inclusion of such directives signals a more serious approach to attaining legislative goals. By specification of facilitating features, legislators provide agency officials with more certainty than the usual vague set of expectations. In addition, the authorization to employ commitment- and capacity-building tools gives agencies the means to help them secure compliance of local governments with policy intent. Finally, legislative authorization of these measures puts pressure on legislators to back expectations with funding.

Not surprisingly, the degree of commitment that agency officials have toward the goals of a given policy also has a noteworthy effect upon the effort that agencies expend in implementing the policy. Increasing agency predisposition to carry out a mandate from the median level of the mandates under study to the seventy-fifth percentile results in an 11 percent increase in implementation effort. Committed agency officials presumably signal to agency personnel that their actions will be monitored. In addition, committed agency officials are also presumably willing to lobby legislators for requisite funding.

However, the capacity of state agencies is neither a statistically nor a substantively noteworthy influence on the implementation effort of state agencies. For the agencies we studied, respondents felt capacity was generally adequate but reported more variability in agency commitment. This is borne out by the data, which show greater variability for agency commitment than for agency capacity. Thus, it may be that we have not adequately captured the threshold for the minimum requisite levels of agency capacity below which effort begins to drop off.

Unlike its effect on implementation style, the mix of provisions authorizing use of coercion or incentives does not have a noteworthy influence on state agency implementation effort. Greater emphasis on coercion might be expected to result in stronger implementation efforts. However, as noted by Gormley (1992), the "get tough" provisions may be sufficiently unclear

---

4. Separate statistical models estimating the individual influence of commitment- and capacity-building features upon implementation effort show an effect for commitment-building with a standardized coefficient of .67 ($p < .01$) and an effect for capacity-building with a standardized coefficient of .65 ($p < .01$). Entering both factors as additive variables in the same model introduces multicollinearity problems.

or agency staff too stretched to apply the called-for sanctions. State agencies may also be reluctant to impose sanctions on local governments when they fear retribution by local officials in lobbying for reductions in agency funding.

One of the more important findings from the perspective of implementation theory is that increases in the clarity of the goals of mandates (and associated decreases in policy complexity) are not associated with stronger agency implementation efforts. This calls into question the statutory coherence hypothesis, which relates more-coherent statutes to ease of implementation and greater agency effort. (Other statistical models, substituting measures of implementation complexity and system change for the clarity of goals, had similar results in failing to detect an influence on agency effort when controlling for other factors.)

It may be that the clarity of goals for the mandates we study is sufficient to prevent a serious blockage to strong implementation. However, we showed earlier in the chapter that the comprehensive-planning mandates had particularly vague goals and complex implementation structures. Why, then, is this not a serious hindrance to the implementation efforts of state agencies? We think that this lack of clarity (and associated complexity of implementation design) is compensated for by other factors. For some planning mandates, such as those found in Florida and to a lesser extent in North Carolina, the confusion created by a lack of statutory coherence is compensated for by the specification of facilitating features (i.e., commitment- and capacity-building provisions) and strong state agency commitment to carrying out the policies.

Discussion and Implications

This chapter has examined how the design of state mandates structures implementation. The study draws attention to differences in policy design among the five states we studied and between comprehensive-planning and single-purpose mandates. The analyses of state agency implementation style and effort provide an understanding of how the differences in mandate design influence the translation of policy into practice.

The comparison of mandate designs among the five states shows the fairly distinct ways the states have gone about the business of shaping the planning and development management policies of local governments. The contrast between California and Florida is one of an older, relatively weak versus a newer, relatively strong approach to comprehensive-planning mandates.

The contrast between Texas and Washington is one of minimalist versus strong single-purpose mandates. Comparing Florida with Washington provides the sharpest contrast in choice between comprehensive planning to address hazards (Florida) and hazard-focused, single-purpose mandates (Washington). North Carolina is of interest because it combines elements of both the old and the new and thereby reflects the transition that many states might face in choosing to implement or reform comprehensive-planning mandates.

The comparison of policy designs for comprehensive-planning and single-purpose mandates suggests refinements concerning commonly held notions about the differences between the two types of mandates. Planning mandates are clearly broader and therefore more complicated to implement. However, the distinctions between the two categories of mandates are not as pointed as often argued in terms of key provisions of the legislation and its implementation. This reinforces our notion that planning and single-purpose mandates reflect different locations on a continuum of approaches to addressing development and hazards. At issue for further analysis in subsequent chapters is the extent to which the implementation complexity of planning mandates is compensated by use of capacity- and commitment-building features aimed at stimulating appropriate local governmental actions.

The analysis of implementation style addresses the character of state agency dealings with local governments. These can range from an informal, flexible approach to a more formal, legalistic approach. Our statistical modeling shows that mandates that include more coercive features instill a more formal, legalistic implementation style. This is consistent with the notion that coercive features set expectations for implementers to "get tough" and provide the means for doing so.

The most noteworthy findings with respect to implementation style are the contingent effects of the commitment and capacity of state agencies upon the approach they adopt in working with local governments. More-cooperative approaches are pursued when the commitment and capacity of relevant state agencies are both strong. But more-formal, legalistic approaches result when the commitment of state agencies is strong and capacity is weak. For other combinations, the effect upon implementation style is negligible. Higher agency commitment and capacity provide greater agency freedom and confidence in pursuing more-cooperative approaches. Higher commitment without commensurate capacity leads to increased procedural formalism.

The analysis of the efforts that state agencies have made to carry out the various mandates shows that policy makers can influence implementation efforts by altering key features of the legislation. In particular, through specification of the actions agencies undertake to build local governmental commitment and capacity, expectations for state agencies are shaped. Also relevant is the commitment of the leadership of state agencies to the policy.

Perhaps the most important finding from this chapter is our failure to find support for the statutory coherence hypothesis linking stronger implementation efforts to less complex, more clearly specified mandates. This suggests that a high degree of statutory coherence—as typically found in single-purpose mandates but not found in comprehensive-planning mandates—is not a necessary condition for successful implementation. It appears that the confusion created by vague goals and complex implementation structures can be compensated for in the design of legislation and through strong commitment by relevant agencies to reaching desired policy goals.

The findings of this chapter show that careful attention to the design of comprehensive-planning and single-purpose mandates can make a difference in state agency implementation efforts and to a lesser extent in state agency implementation styles. In this regard, this chapter draws attention to specification of the facilitating features built into mandates that are aimed at building the commitment of local governments to state goals and building their capacity to pursue those goals. As the complexity of mandates increases, it is crucial that strong signals about implementation expectations be sent via appropriate inclusion of these features.

7

Enhancing Planning

Skeptics have raised a number of important questions about planning mandates: Do planning mandates really have an effect on local governments? Aren't local governments in the dozens of states without mandates just as likely to prepare comprehensive plans as those that are under the thumb of state government? Aren't the plans local governments produce in response to mandates likely to be mere exercises, not really worth the paper on which they are printed? And what use are plans anyway—do they really have any power to sway how people and (as important) public officials think about urban growth and development?

These questions reflect widespread skepticism in the United States about the value of planning and about the ability of states to affect local policy about urban growth and development. At times that skepticism has been translated into federal policy, as when the federal government, after investing heavily in local government planning for twenty-five years, in 1981 completely scrapped its planning assistance program. It is also reflected in the slow diffusion of the planning mandate idea. Thirty years after Hawaii became the first state to launch a comprehensive state growth management program, only a dozen states have adopted planning mandates. The reluctance of the states to use mandates as a policy tool, we suspect, is due in some measure to the complete lack of credible evidence about their worth.

Here we provide answers to the skeptics' questions. In contrast to much conventional wisdom—in government and in academia—we find two things. First, when crafted correctly, mandates have a tangible impact on both the amount and the quality of local planning. Second, if plans are of high-enough quality, they have a measurable effect on the willingness of public officials to manage urban growth to achieve important state policy objectives. To explain how these have occurred, we turn first to theory and revisit our review in chapter 1 of what advocates have claimed for plans. We then provide evidence we obtained about what actually has transpired in the communities in California, Florida, North Carolina, Texas, and Washington where we studied local plans and interviewed planning professionals.

The Planning Idea

Comprehensive plans are one means of formalizing the identification of community needs and pointing the way toward more effective, efficient, and equitable use of community resources in meeting those needs. In the case of natural hazards, which provide the basis for our evaluation of the efficacy of plans, the knowledge plans assemble is supposed to help local governments identify risks and find feasible ways in which risks can be reduced. Information about local problems also may increase governmental commitment to finding solutions. When comprehensive plans are prepared or updated, local officials have an opportunity to evaluate problems and weigh alternative solutions. Improved understanding of local conditions and potential solutions should raise awareness and commitment to take action.

Plans may enhance prospects for community decision making about hazard-prone areas in two ways. First, they can improve the level of understanding and the technical capacity of government decision makers. Second, they can catalyze political constituencies outside government, which, in turn, demand attention to problems that previously were ignored. Plans, for example, can provide information on the location and magnitude of hazards and can alert elected officials to the potential costs of permitting public and private development in such areas. Plans also may increase the likelihood that local officials will consider the most appropriate use of hazardous areas, limiting development intensities where the risks of catastrophic losses are highest.

In spite of these potential benefits, local governments frequently have failed to initiate plan making on their own or, once they have prepared plans, to keep them current. The payoffs from planning are remote in time, while the political costs of limiting urban growth or increasing costs through higher design standards are immediate. Thus, when staff resources are allocated, they tend to be devoted to immediate problems that require attention and to day-to-day administration of zoning and other land use regulations, not to preparation and maintenance of long-range plans. State comprehensive-planning mandates seek to overcome these constraints in order to induce planning where it otherwise would be ignored and to foster higher-quality plans. In the previous chapter, we discussed various tools the states have used to persuade local governments to prepare plans. The states' goal, however, is production not of mere "paper" plans but of ones that are of high-enough quality to actually inform and influence policy decisions about urban development.

Improving the Quality of Plans

A key goal of planning mandates is better-quality local plans. But plan quality is difficult to define. Practicing planners can differentiate high-quality plans from low-quality ones, but they are hard-pressed to identify explicitly the defining characteristics of a good plan. The planning literature is surprisingly sparse when it comes to describing what constitutes a superior plan. Planners generally avoid this normative question and focus instead on plan-making methods and processes.

Nevertheless, there have been several important attempts to define the characteristics of high-quality plans (see Chapin and Kaiser 1979; Hollander et al. 1988; Kent 1991). From these efforts a basic consensus has evolved about the features of plans that most influence development decisions made by local governments. The effort by planning educators Chapin and Kaiser (1979, 327-40) perhaps best defines the characteristics to be considered. The authors discuss three critical components of comprehensive plans. First, the factual underpinnings of the plan describe and analyze social, economic, and environmental conditions and trends related to the growth and development of the community. Second, goals identify general aspirations of the population, problems needing alleviation, and needs that are premised on shared values of community members. Third, policies and recommended actions serve as guides to decisions about the amount, location, design, and timing of public and private development to insure that progress is made toward achieving the goals specified in the plan. A few studies have evaluated different types of plans and their impacts on decisions made by local governments. They provide some clues about the characteristics of a plan that affect its usefulness to decision makers.

Planning researcher Richard Fishman (1978) evaluated housing and land use elements of comprehensive plans in twenty-seven cities. He concluded that the best plans contain specific goals (e.g., preservation of neighborhoods and provision of balanced housing) that are linked to local conditions rather than general goals (e.g., protection of human, economic, and physical assets and greater governmental responsiveness) that lack specificity. He concluded that policies stated in plans should be action oriented and should use words like "will" or "must" rather than less-guiding language like "might" or "could." Development proposals in the cities Fishman studied were more likely to be consistent with plans that contained specific substantive goals and policies.

Stephen Pitkin (1992), a practicing planner in Florida, assessed the evolution of different plans in the city of Sunrise, Florida, over a twenty-year period. He found that, compared with low-quality plans, high-quality plans were used more frequently as a reference document for data and policies during planning board and council meetings and for the preparation of land development codes and other planning documents. A key distinction between high- and low-quality plans was that high-quality plans contained data and analysis to justify the objectives and policies they proposed, whereas low-quality plans did not.

In another noteworthy study, planning educator Charles Connerly (1990) analyzed housing elements of plans in ten Florida communities. He gives several explanations for the frequent use of good plans. First, good plans include a sound analysis of existing conditions based on a detailed inventory of local housing stocks and assessments of current and projected housing needs and supplies. Second, they have goals that address a range of housing needs. Third, they contain policies that are stated clearly and are specific to each goal. The policies also identify funding sources and specify a time frame for their implementation.

In summary, a literature examining the quality of comprehensive plans has begun to accumulate. There seems to be consensus that the quality of comprehensive plans depends on the degree to which (1) facts are employed to define and analyze local problems and needs; (2) goals are clearly stated and are comprehensive; and (3) alternative policies are specific and action oriented. These three characteristics are the dimensions we employed in our evaluation of local plans.

The specific indicators we used are listed in the table below. The fact basis dimension consists of an index composed of ratings of the mapping, emergency planning, and exposure features of plans. The goals dimension combines ratings of hazards and environmental objectives. The policies dimension is an index based on ratings of policies related to creating awareness of hazards, regulating building, site design, and land use, creating incentives for safe development practices in hazardous areas, providing infrastructure to control hazards and design standards for public facilities, delineating postdisaster recovery procedures, and specifying measures for emergency preparedness. (The details regarding these indexes are provided in the methodological appendix.)

Components of Plan Quality

Fact Basis Dimension
  Map information
    Delineation of location of hazard
    Delineation of magnitude of hazard
  Emergency response data
    Emergency shelter demand and capacity
    Evacuation and clearance time data
  Exposure data
    Number of current population exposed
    Number of public infrastructures exposed
    Value of private structures exposed
    Number of critical facilities exposed
    Loss estimates for private structures
    Loss estimates for public structures
Goals Dimension
  Hazard-related goals
    Reduction of property losses
    Protection of population safety
    Reduction of damage to private property
    Minimization of fiscal impacts of disasters
    Equitable distribution of hazard program costs
    Promotion of hazards awareness
  Environmental goals
    Preservation of natural areas as part of reduction of hazard losses
    Preservation of open space and recreation areas as part of reduction of hazard losses
    Maintenance of good water quality as part of reduction of hazard losses
Policies Dimension
  Awareness policies
    Educational awareness
    Voluntary real estate disclosure of hazard
    Disaster warning and response
    Posting of signs delineating hazardous areas
    Encouragement of hazard insurance purchase
    Technical assistance about mitigation actions
  Regulatory Policies
    Permitted land uses
    Density of land use

Components of Plan Quality, (*continued*)

  Transfer of development rights
  Cluster development
  Setbacks
  Site review
  Special study/impact assessment
  Building standards
  Mandatory real estate disclosure of hazard
  Land or property acquisition
  Financing of mitigation projects
  Mandatory retrofitting of private structures
Incentives policies
  Voluntary retrofitting of private structures
  Voluntary land and property acquisition
  Tax abatement for using mitigation
  Density bonus
  Low-interest loans for retrofitting buildings
Infrastructure Policies
  Structural controls
  Capital improvement adjustments
  Retrofitting public infrastructure
  Addressing critical facilities
Recovery Policies
  Land use changes
  Building design changes
  Moratorium on new construction
  Establishment of a recovery organization
  Capital improvement adjustments
  Private acquisition and relocation
  Financing recovery programs
Preparedness policies
  Evacuation provisions
  Sheltering provisions
  Requirements for emergency plans

Mandates, Plans, and Plan Quality

We studied eighty-eight local governments in California, Florida, and North Carolina that were mandated to prepare comprehensive plans. Each of the eighty-eight governments complied with the relevant provisions of the state mandate and, in fact, prepared and adopted a plan.

The experience in producing plans is mixed for the three comparison areas where local plans are not mandated by state policy. Comprehensive plans had been prepared by fewer than half of the local governments we studied in the North Carolina mountain area and in the state of Texas. In Washington, however, most local governments had plans. Thus, in some states local governments will prepare comprehensive plans without the state telling them to do so. We think the Washington state planning experience reflects a more progressive and environmentally conscious ethos about land resources than is found in most states. In less progressive states like North Carolina and Texas, unless the state directs them to plan, many local governments will manage urban growth in an ad hoc way, based on the pressures of the moment rather than on systematic analysis of local conditions, clear goals, or policy alternatives—that is, without preparing a plan to guide their development management decisions. Thus, the answer to one of the questions skeptics have raised about mandates is clear. Local governments are more likely to prepare comprehensive plans when state comprehensive-planning mandates exist than when the state leaves preparation of a plan solely to the discretion of local governments.

State comprehensive-planning mandates also result in higher-quality local plans. Here we review these impacts by comparing the fact, goal, and policy attributes of plans prepared by eighty-eight local governments subject to state mandates with the fact, goal, and policy attributes of plans prepared by fifty-two local governments that were not subject to mandates.

The scores evaluating plan quality, summarized in figure 7.1, demonstrate that state planning mandates result in plans that are far superior in quality to plans prepared in states without mandates. Every aspect of plan quality we examined—facts, goals, policies, and overall quality—is better. The figure also shows, however, that on average neither group of plans does a very good job of addressing natural hazards. The indexes we calculated have a possible range from 0, indicating absolutely no mention of natural hazards in a plan, to 5, indicating a plan that incorporates all of the fact, goal, and policy dimensions we scored. In the state with the highest-quality plans (North Carolina), the average total plan quality score is only 1.35 of a possible 5 points.

Among the three states with planning mandates, local governments in North Carolina prepared plans that are superior to those in California and Florida. Part of that difference is due to the state of North Carolina's insistence in the mid-1980s that local governments pay attention to hurricane hazards in required five-year updates of their comprehensive plans. That led to considerable attention among coastal localities to the factual underpinnings of their plans, which are much more likely than plans found in other states to have detailed maps of land exposed to hazards, information on emergency shelters and evacuation routes and times, and estimates of

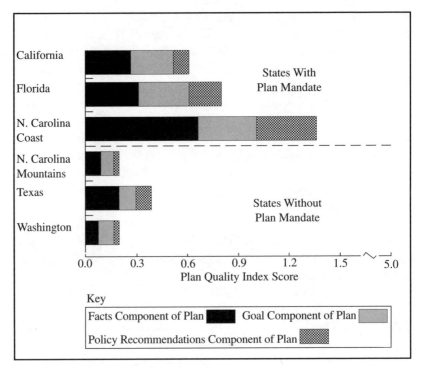

FIGURE 7.1 Plan Quality

population and property at risk. With stronger factual and analytic under-pinnings, plans in North Carolina tend to propose significantly more reme-dial and preventive actions than plans prepared by local governments in other states.

In addition, however, the superior plans in North Carolina (and also Florida) came about because these states made strong efforts to build local capacity and commitment. The outcomes of their efforts are illustrated by the opinions of city and county planning directors. We asked planning direc-tors to rate four state initiatives in terms of their effects on the quality of lo-cal plans. The state initiatives we asked about are (1) preparation of maps that delineate hazardous areas (an example of state efforts to improve local capacity to plan), (2) provision of technical data about potential losses from natural hazards (another example of capacity building), (3) review of and comment on drafts of the local plan (a technique to increase local commit-ment to follow state dictates as well as to aid local capacity to produce a good plan), and (4) financial assistance for the preparation of the plan (also a tech-nique to build both commitment and capacity). The percentages of planning directors who rated each as an important influence on the attention given to

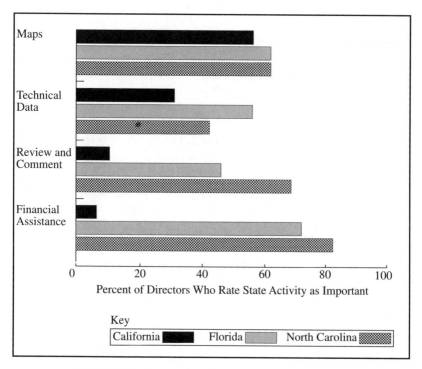

FIGURE 7.2 Importance of State Actions to Plan Quality

natural hazards in the plans prepared by their governments are shown in figure 7.2.

The figure clearly illustrates a key point. The commitment-building features of mandates most clearly differentiate Florida and North Carolina, with their higher-quality local government plans, from California, with its relatively lower-quality plans. North Carolina localities prepared plans that rated highest by our scoring methods, and, not coincidentally, North Carolina planning directors were most likely to cite state review of their plans and state financial assistance as an important contribution to their planning efforts. Florida stands in an intermediate position, but California lags far behind, reflecting the relatively passive role of state officials there in implementing the state planning mandate and the failure of California to offer financial assistance and other incentives to foster higher-quality local plans.

State efforts to build local capacity through the provision of technical assistance such as maps delineating hazard zones also had an effect on the quality of local planning. As the figure shows, a majority of planning directors in each state thought state-provided maps were important in helping them produce better plans, and a number also cited other types of technical assistance as important. But state-provided technical assistance does not account for the differences across states in the quality of local plans, since each state provided equivalent amounts of assistance.

We theorized in chapter 1 that differences across local governments in situational factors, such as the wealth needed to finance government programs, would result in variation in the quality of the local plans produced. By looking separately at local governments that were subject and not subject to a state planning mandate, we are able to test for the effects of situational factors independent of the effects of the presence or absence of the planning mandate. Local governments not subject to a state mandate tend to produce higher-quality plans when they have more resources (wealth) and when the problem is more tractable to solution through land use management (as indicated by relatively low economic demand for land in hazardous areas and low population pressure). Other factors we examined—the size of the community and seriousness of previous losses in natural disasters, for example—do not differentiate localities that produce low-quality plans from those that produce high-quality plans.[1]

For localities in states with mandates, we found a similar pattern. Wealthier communities produced higher-quality plans in California, Florida, and North Carolina. But that is the only situational factor that has any detectable effect on the quality of local plans prepared in those states.[2] Apparently, when state officials make an effort to convince local policy makers to prepare good plans, their demands override factors such as high economic demand for land in hazardous areas that otherwise make the formulation of good plans difficult. As with the localities in states without planning mandates, in the states with mandates we found no effects on plan quality from variation

1. Readers should note, however, that the overall model is not statistically significant. Therefore, an alternative conclusion would be that plan quality in the absence of a state planning mandate is due to other factors we did not model, such as the existence of some idiosyncratic factor that for some reason leads planners to attend to natural hazards. Our analysis involved ordinary least squares regression using procedures contained in the Systat statistical package. Variables we examined are those previous research suggests should explain attention to natural hazards in planning. The adjusted coefficient of determination for the regression model is .01 ($F = 0.75$, $p < .63$, $N = 52$). The standardized regression coefficients for the model are: demand for land in hazard areas, $-.28$ ($p < .10$); wealth, .27 ($p < .10$); population growth from 1980 to 1990, $-.26$ ($p < .10$); repetitively flooded property, .13 ($p > .10$); size of hazard area, .02 ($p > .10$); 1990 population, $-.09$ ($p > .10$); and catastrophic losses since 1970, $-.05$ ($p > .10$).

2. In the case of the three states with planning mandates, the strength of the mandate overwhelmed local situational factors in affecting variation in the quality of local plans. This statistical analysis also involved ordinary least squares regression. The adjusted coefficient of determination is .48 ($F = 9.87$, $p < .001$). The standardized regression coefficients for the model are: North Carolina coast dummy variable, .93 ($p < .001$); Florida

in the strength of the single-purpose state mandates discussed in the preceding chapter. In preparing plans, localities apparently take all of their signals about what the plan should address and how it should be prepared from the planning mandate.

The Impact of Plans on Commitment to State Objectives

The commitment of local officials to accomplish state policy objectives occupies a critical intervening role in our theorizing. Mandates and the local plans they require are not ends in themselves but tools to persuade and enable local officials to embrace state policy objectives. Armed with greater commitment and understanding of policy problems, we believe local governments will then undertake various programs to accomplish state policy ends.

Commitment is the degree to which local governments subscribe to the objectives sought by mandates and are willing to work toward their achievement (May and Williams 1986). This is sometimes referred to as normative commitment in the social control literature (see Balch 1980; Etzioni 1961; Wood 1974). Previous research on natural hazards has found local commitment to be particularly problematic. In the mid-1970s, for example, sociologist Peter Rossi and his colleagues surveyed two thousand leaders in state and local government and the private sector to find out how concerned they were about a variety of natural hazards. The group concluded: "For the most part, political decision makers in the states and local communities do not see environmental hazards as a very serious problem" (Rossi, Wright, and Weber-Burdin 1982, 9). Other researchers have found direct links between low commitment and local government failure to address flood hazards, coastal storm and hurricane hazards, and seismic safety (see Burby and French 1985; Godschalk, Brower, and Beatley 1989; and Berke and Beatley 1992). Thus, to policy analysts William Petak and Arthur Atkisson, "The primary impediment to the adoption and enforcement of effective natural hazards regulatory policy. . . [is the lack of] 'willingness' rather than [of] 'capacity' of governmental law-making bodies to act" (Petak and Atkisson 1982, 422).

We found that state planning mandates and the plans they engender have a measurable, stimulating effect on the commitment of local officials to state

---

dummy variable, .32 ($p < .01$); wealth, .16 ($p < .10$); population growth from 1980 to 1990, .09 ($p > .10$); catastrophic losses since 1970, $-.06$ ($p > .10$); repetitively flooded property, .05 ($p > .10$); demand for land in hazard areas, .04 ($p > .10$); and 1990 population, $-.03$ ($p > .10$).

policy goals. But in the case of natural hazards, the effect is indirect and operates through the knowledge that plans build about natural hazards and the political demands that knowledge fosters rather than directly from technical analyses of hazards as a policy problem. This reflects the key function of plans and planning processes in communicating with stakeholders (groups potentially affected by hazards) so that they understand the problems that face them. Planning also involves going one step further and actually working with groups to find acceptable solutions (see Forester 1989; Innes 1995). The state planning mandates we studied recognize this. An important feature of each mandate is a requirement that citizens participate in the planning process.

In addition, plans can empower citizens to become active in demanding governmental attention to community problems. In the case of natural hazards, this is a noteworthy effect, because hazards are a particularly difficult type of policy problem. Political scientist Peter Huber calls such hazards "public risks" because they are "broadly distributed, often temporally remote, and largely outside the individual risk bearer's direct understanding and control" (Huber 1986, 90). Most people, including policy makers, do not perceive public risks accurately and tend to dismiss them as trivial nuisances not worthy of serious public attention.

The information provided in plans helps citizens and government decision makers appreciate the true threat posed by public risks such as natural hazards. By actively involving citizens in the planning process, planners develop consensus about how vulnerability can be reduced in a way that is acceptable to most affected parties (see Kaiser, Godschalk, and Chapin 1995). Thus, plans based on participation can stimulate citizen attention to the problems the plan addresses and to make political demands for governmental action.

Evidence that these effects exist in practice is provided in figure 7.3. The figure presents a summary of the results from statistical modeling that shows paths linking state mandates and the quality of comprehensive plans with stakeholder knowledge of natural hazards and the political demands they make and to the commitment of planning staff and elected officials to hazard mitigation.[3] The larger the coefficient (indicated by the thickness of the line

3. The path model illustrated in figure 7.3 is constructed from the results of a series of least squares regression analyses. These model results are summarized here for each of the dependent variables along the paths leading from state mandates to the commitment of planning staff and elected officials to address natural hazards.

Plan quality. The adjusted coefficient of determination is .25 (F = 6.33, p < .000, N = 176). Standardized regression coefficients are: California dummy variable, .07 (p > .05); Florida dummy variable, .37 (p < .001); North Carolina coast dummy variable, .57

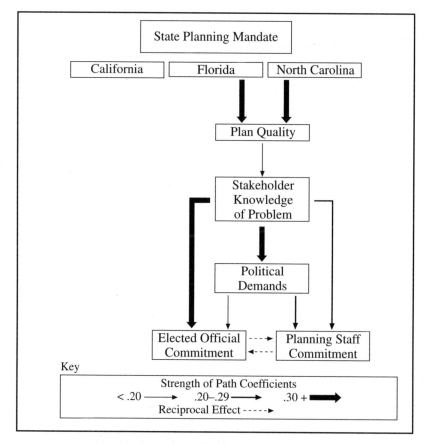

FIGURE 7.3 Path Model of Plans and Commitment
NOTE: Controlling for size of hazard area, demand for land in hazard area, degree of experience with repetitive losses, magnitude of previous natural disasters, population, 1990, growth 1980–90, and median home value.

in the figure), the stronger the effect of a particular factor in the chain of cause and effect illustrated. The path model was constructed using statistical controls for the effects of other factors that can influence the quality of plans, knowledge of stakeholders about hazards, political demands, and

($p < .001$); Texas dummy variable, .11 ($p > .05$); size of hazard area, .09 ($p > .10$); demand for land in hazard area, $-.001$ ($p > .05$); repetitively flooded property, .06 ($p > .05$); catastrophic losses since 1970, $-.18$ ($p < .01$); 1990 population, $-.001$ ($p > .05$); population growth from 1980 to 1990, .12 ($p < .05$); wealth, .21 ($p < .05$).

Stakeholder knowledge of problem. The adjusted coefficient of determination is .16 ($F = 3.67$, $p < .000$, N = 176). Standardized regression coefficients are: California dummy variable, .14 ($p > .05$); Florida dummy variable, .30 ($p < .01$); North Carolina commitment. These controls include various indicators of the seriousness of the threat posed by natural hazards and the capacity of the jurisdiction to deal with this problem.

Figure 7.3 shows that higher-quality plans result in greater knowledge and more understanding of natural hazards among stakeholders. Our interviews with local planners also provided evidence of this effect of plans. For example, in jurisdictions with plans of above-average quality, our informants estimated (on average) that almost 60 percent of the residents and developers living and working in these communities had a good understanding of threats posed by natural hazards. In jurisdictions that lacked plans or had plans that scored below the median in plan quality, less than half of the stakeholders (on average) were viewed by our local informants as knowl-

---

coast dummy variable, .26 ($p < .01$); Texas dummy variable, .50 ($p < .001$); plan quality, .18 ($p < .05$); size of hazard area, .16 ($p < .05$); demand for land in hazard area, .08 ($p > .05$); repetitively flooded property, $-.07$ ($p > .05$); catastrophic losses since 1970, .07 ($p > .05$); 1990 population, .02 ($p > .05$); population growth from 1980 to 1990, .05 ($p > .05$); wealth, $-.07$ ($p > .05$).

Political demands for solutions. The adjusted coefficient of determination is .24 ($F = 5.14$, $p < .000$, $N = 176$). Standardized regression coefficients are: California dummy variable, $-.11$ ($p > .05$); Florida dummy variable, $-.10$ ($p > .05$); North Carolina coast dummy variable, $-.13$ ($p > .05$); Texas dummy variable, .07 ($p > .05$); plan quality, .09 ($p > .05$); stakeholder knowledge of problem, .30 ($p < .001$); size of hazard area, $-.16$ ($p < .05$); demand for land in hazard area, .35 ($p < .001$); repetitively flooded property, .07 ($p > .05$); catastrophic losses since 1970, .01 ($p > .05$); 1990 population, .08 ($p > .05$); population growth from 1980 to 1990, .14 ($p < .05$); wealth, .02 ($p > .05$).

Planning staff commitment to hazard mitigation. The adjusted coefficient of determination is .09 ($F = 2.22$, $p < .009$, $N = 172$). Standardized regression coefficients are: California dummy variable, $-.10$ ($p > .05$); Florida dummy variable, $-.03$ ($p > .05$); North Carolina coast dummy variable, $-.16$ ($p > .05$); Texas dummy variable, $-.11$ ($p > .05$); plan quality, .02 ($p > .05$); stakeholder knowledge of problem, .20 ($p < .01$); political demands for solutions, .24 ($p < .01$); size of hazard area, .09 ($p > .05$); demand for land in hazard area, $-.17$ ($p < .05$); repetitively flooded property, .05 ($p > .05$); catastrophic losses since 1970, .04 ($p > .05$); 1990 population, $-.003$ ($p > .05$); population growth from 1980 to 1990, .02 ($p > .05$); wealth, .16 ($p > .05$).

Elected official commitment to hazard mitigation. The adjusted coefficient of determination is .28 ($F = 5.80$, $p < .001$, $N = 175$). Standardized regression coefficients are: California dummy variable, $-.26$ ($p < .01$); Florida dummy variable, $-.13$ ($p > .05$); North Carolina coast dummy variable, $-.07$ ($p > .05$); Texas dummy variable, .09 ($p > .05$); plan quality, $-.003$ ($p > .05$); stakeholder knowledge of problem, .38 ($p < .001$); political demands for solutions, .15 ($p < .05$); size of hazard area, .11 ($p > .05$); demand for land in hazard area, $-.21$ ($p < .05$); repetitively flooded property, .09 ($p > .05$); catastrophic losses since 1970, .01 ($p > .05$); 1990 population, $-.05$ ($p > .05$); population growth from 1980 to 1990, $-.01$ ($p > .05$); wealth, .26 ($p < .01$).

edgeable about hazards. As stakeholders develop a greater understanding of hazards through the planning process, both planning staff and elected officials come to also learn about this issue and to become more committed to doing something about it.

In addition, the more knowledgeable stakeholders become, the more likely that are to act politically on that knowledge. These political acts—asking public officials directly to take action and attending meetings and serving on committees to secure action—also have a marked effect on the commitment to hazard reduction of planning staff and elected officials. What is more, the political messages officials receive may be far different in communities with plans.

We found that both environmental and neighborhood groups are twice as likely to demand attention to natural hazards in communities with plans than in communities without plans and that the level of their activism then actually exceeds that of business interests (although the difference is not statistically significant). By way of contrast, in communities without plans, business groups are twice as likely as environmental or neighborhood groups to be trying to affect local policy toward natural hazards. Thus, the knowledge that plans generate and share with stakeholders clearly broadens the scope of local political discourse about natural hazards and how to deal with them.

Finally, once planning staff and elected officials become committed to doing something about hazards, they affect the commitment of each other. The planning staff helps get the issue on the local policy agenda, and elected officials committed to dealing with the issue ask the staff to formulate policy proposals for additional action. In the following chapter, we extend this chain by one additional link, showing that commitment has a strong impact on the quality of the development management programs local governments subsequently formulate.

Discussion and Implications

The analyses presented in this chapter permit an initial answer to the question of how important state comprehensive-planning mandates are to the strength of local plans and the commitment of local officials to state policy objectives. Our findings indicate that local governments responding to a state comprehensive-planning mandate are more likely to have prepared comprehensive plans and to have higher-quality plans than local governments in states without a mandate. In short, state planning mandates are an important factor in determining the quality of local comprehensive plans.

The factual information and analysis found in plans that were produced in response to state mandates are stronger than that found in plans prepared by local governments in states without mandates. This is because state planning mandates encourage local governments to develop better information regarding hazards and to include it in their planning process. State planning mandates also encourage greater attention in local plans to goals for reducing potential loss from disasters. The differences between the strength of hazard-related policies proposed in the state-mandated and nonmandated local plans are striking. The plans of states without mandates contain very limited policy recommendations. In contrast, the state-mandated plans contain much stronger policy recommendations.

However, adoption of a state planning mandate does not guarantee high-quality plans. Even in states with planning mandates, the quality of the hazards elements of comprehensive plans is generally weak. Our empirical analyses suggest that differences in plan quality for localities subject to state planning mandates are explained in large part by differences in mandate design and implementation. High-quality plans are fostered by state mandates that contain more-extensive features designed to build commitment and capacity to local planning. These include grants-in-aid for the preparation of plans, state review of plans for consistency with policy objectives and standards, and adequate sanctions for local governments that fail to comply with state requirements. In communities not subject to state planning mandates, plan quality is affected by affluence and the tractability of land use management as a way to deal with hazards. Surprisingly, we did not detect any effects on plan quality of single-purpose, functional mandates (such as California's seismic safety laws or Florida's shoreline protection programs). Apparently, these functional mandates do not "spill over" and influence how comprehensive plans are prepared.

In the absence of a planning process, political demands for attention to hazard mitigation tend to arise primarily from pressures to develop unsafe areas. That may tend to push governmental action toward measures such as stream channelization and levees that make previously undevelopable land suitable for urban use. The same result may arise from political demands for action that emerge in the wake of a disaster, but among the communities we studied, there is no difference in the degree of demand that interest groups assert for attention to hazards among communities that have and have not experienced a previous disaster. Possibly, disaster-inspired demands for action are short-lived. Whether driven by hopes for profit from future development or for protection of existing development, the environmental consequences of trying to reduce risk by managing the hazard can be devastating,

for example, as streams are channelized and shorelines are fortified to reduce flooding and erosion.

State planning mandates take the place of necessary, but often absent, local situational factors that induce local government planners and elected
officials to pay attention to natural hazards. If states require local planning in
a forceful manner (as in Florida and North Carolina), local obstacles to planning become less significant. Instead, plan quality becomes highly dependent on what the mandate requires. Strong political coalitions that are
progrowth may still be present and opposed to efforts that restrict development opportunities in hazardous areas. But state planning mandates help local governments overcome such opposition and can foster political support
for approaches to dealing with hazards that are environmentally sustain-
able. Planning mandates also can help to replace dependence on local resources for preparing plans, if state resources are devoted to building local
planning capacity. Without such capacity building, local governments serving less affluent communities do not have the resources to devote to hazard
mitigation and can not overcome political coalitions that promote growth at
all costs.

In sum, the analyses presented in this chapter make clear that state planning mandates do matter. They affect the structure, content, and quality of
local plans. Higher-quality plans in turn affect the commitment of local officials to state policy goals such as hazard mitigation. As a consequence, state
planning mandates are a potentially powerful policy tool the states can use to
influence the decisions that local governments make about urban growth
and development.

8

Managing Development

High-quality plans do not automatically translate into strong development management programs. Conversely, strong development management programs do not necessarily require that comprehensive plans be in place first. Chapter 7 examined the role of state mandates in enhancing the quality of plans and building local commitment to pursue state policy objectives. In this chapter, we look at local governmental decisions to implement plans and to formulate programs to manage development in such a way as to reduce losses from natural hazards.

Reducing or mitigating human and property losses inevitably involves the management of the physical development of a community. Such management applies both to public infrastructure and to private development. It may focus on the hazard itself (e.g., by stabilizing slopes and providing flood retention basins), thereby reducing the risk to public and private property. Or it may attempt to make public and private development less vulnerable (e.g., by land use and building standards). It may be anticipatory (e.g., limiting development in hazard-prone areas), remedial (e.g., retrofitting existing structures), or emergency oriented (e.g., establishing evacuation routes).

We classify different strategies into six distinctive areas of development management: land use, site design, building design, knowledge enhancement, structural protection from hazards, and protection of community facilities. The first four of these focus on methods that directly affect private property. The last two strategies involve public property and investments. Historically, approaches to hazard mitigation have mainly entailed extensive public investment in structural measures to protect public and private property, along with building standards and site design requirements to protect individual structures. In developed areas, many of these building requirements are remedial (e.g., retrofitting masonry buildings to better withstand earthquakes). Recent efforts have turned to a more preventive or anticipatory approach, whereby flexible site design limits construction on the vulnerable portions of a property or creative land use planning limits development altogether in hazard-prone areas. Knowledge-building approaches may be either anticipatory, warning of hazards, or remedial, explaining how to retrofit buildings to reduce risk. Public property protection is a special case, in that community facilities and infrastructure may be retrofitted, designed initially to reduce vulnerability, or located so as not to inadvertently encourage private development in hazard-prone areas.

Land use controls and site design requirements are more oriented toward planning than the more traditional building standards or structural protection measures. This distinction is conceptually important as the latter approaches permit, and may even encourage, development in hazard-prone areas by appearing to make them safer (at least up to a minimum level). In contrast, the land use controls and site design requirements discourage development altogether or locate it more carefully to avoid exposure to hazards.

In this chapter, we pay particular attention to the choices governments make among these development management techniques and strategies, contrasting various land use strategies with each other and with strategies that use public information and control of infrastructure to accomplish policy aims. We address development management at two levels. First, we examine the degree to which policy recommendations made in comprehensive plans are subsequently adopted by policy makers. Second, we look at the formulation of development management programs composed of strategies recommended in plans but derived from other sources as well. Thus, we examine the extent to which "paper plans" are converted into programs of action and evaluate the relative importance of plans as a source of ideas for the overall development management programs communities pursue.

Implementing Comprehensive Plans

One way of evaluating the efficacy of plan making is to examine the degree to which the policy recommendations made by local plans are actually acted upon by local governments (Talen 1996 provides a review of previous research on this question). However, the idea of implementation as a gauge for evaluating the efficacy of planning has been criticized on the grounds that it ignores the adaptive nature of public policy. Many policies are no sooner put in place than they are modified to reflect policy learning and changing circumstances. As a result, planning theorist Andreas Faludi argues, plans and the policy recommendations they embody should not be viewed as something that is implemented or carried out but instead as "something to be used when taking decisions about action" (Faludi 1987, 208). From this perspective, the plan is not a problem-solving document but is meant to be a frame-setting document that helps policy makers understand their situation (also see Alexander 1992). This suggests that flexibility is important and implementation cannot be evaluated simply by looking at the number of recommendations that have been acted upon. For example, some time after a plan is adopted development management strategies different from those proposed in the plan may be seen as preferable. There may be new information available, or changing political demands may override the specifics of outdated plans.

Planning can also be viewed as a process of conflict resolution emphasizing consensus building and communication of information. From this perspective, the actions proposed in a plan, if any, are not critical in and of themselves. What is required is that the plan develop a common frame of reference that later can serve decision making (Sager 1990). Planning theory terms this perspective communicative rationality. As we saw in the previous chapter, better plans communicate with stakeholders and build a political constituency for attention to community problems such as natural hazards. That, some planning theorists (e.g., Forester 1989) would argue, may be all that should be asked of plans.

Each of these perspectives has value, but there also is merit in examining the degree to which the recommendations made in plans are acted upon. Most plans, after all, are still written as guides to action. The communicative and procedural aspects of plan making have been increasingly recognized and institutionalized as elements for building consensus. Yet such consensus must be built around not only an understanding but a direction. Even if plans act primarily as frame-setting devices, actions will follow, and as a consequence plans should still indirectly influence the character of development management programs. For these reasons, plan implementation can be evaluated in terms of the consistency between the recommendations made in a plan and actions taken to effectuate these recommendations.

A high proportion of the proposals put forward in the 140 plans we examined—over 60 percent of those aimed at private property—were actually

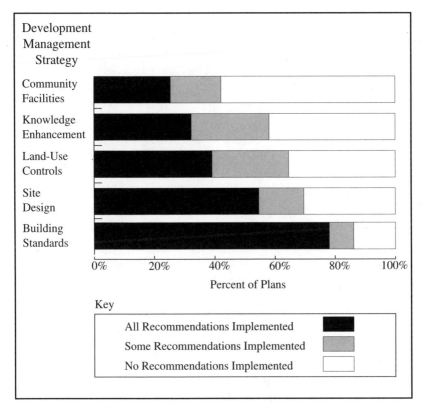

FIGURE 8.1 Extent of Plan Implementation

implemented.[1] As illustrated in figure 8.1, the degree of implementation is highest for proposed changes in building standards to mitigate the effects of hazards, for which five out of every six plan recommendations were subsequently adopted. But over half of even the more politically controversial land use policy measures were adopted. Success of implementation was lowest for proposals dealing with community facilities. We suspect the high costs of the latter measures and the need for cost sharing by other governmental units account for this finding.

Overall, a remarkably high proportion (32 percent) of the plans with recommendations for hazards policy affecting private property were com-

---

1. Success of implementation is gauged by the existence of a regulation or other development management activity that was proposed in a prior local plan.

pletely implemented. Only 10 percent of the plans were merely paper plans for which no recommendations were subsequently adopted. Policy recommendations dealing with community facilities fared the poorest, with 60 percent of the recommendations in local plans lying fallow.

The strong consistency requirements of Florida's planning mandate are reflected in plan implementation. Nearly 70 percent of the proposals for hazard mitigation made by local plans in Florida were acted upon. The corresponding implementation rates in California and North Carolina were lower, 55 and 59 percent respectively. The highest rates of implementation were found in two of the states not subject to state comprehensive-planning mandates. Local plan recommendations in Texas, with a 73 percent success rate, and local plans in Washington, with an 80 percent success rate, tended to be implemented at an even higher rate than those in the states with comprehensive-planning mandates.

The higher success rates in Texas and Washington are an artifact of the lower number of recommendations made by plans in these states and of the fact that not all jurisdictions prepared plans. That is, voluntarily produced plans that put forward a few politically safe recommendations can be implemented more easily than more robust plans. But the higher rates of plan implementation in Texas and Washington did not offset the relatively weak plans local governments prepared. That is, the marginally higher rate of implementation in Texas and Washington multiplied by a much lower number of policy recommendations in plans in these states results in a lower total number of recommendations adopted. A typical local government adopted fewer hazard mitigation measures proposed in plans in Texas (1.2 policies adopted, on average) and Washington (0.8 policies adopted, on average) than a typical local government in California (2.1 policies adopted), Florida (2.8 policies adopted), and the North Carolina coast (2.4 policies adopted). The plans of local governments in the North Carolina mountains contained no policy recommendations for hazard mitigation, so their implementation rate was zero and their ultimate score for policy adoption was also zero.

Factors Affecting Implementation

Multivariate statistical analysis was undertaken to isolate key factors that foster or stifle the implementation of policy recommendations put forward in plans. As was true for the commitment to hazard mitigation by planning staff and elected officials (see chapter 7), political pressure to do something about hazards is a key factor affecting plan implementation.[2] Plans are more likely to be converted from paper plans to actual programs when there is a local constituency for addressing problems posed by hazards. The degree of intractability of the hazard problem also has a noteworthy effect on the extent of plan implementation. As development and density increase, the ability to make use of many anticipatory development management measures is limited. Thus, as density increases not only are there likely to be fewer recommendations made in plans, but those recommendations are also less likely to be implemented.

The overall quality of the comprehensive plan and strength of single-purpose mandates appear to have fairly strong effects on implementation, but our statistical models are not conclusive about this. Higher-quality plans containing more information, stronger analyses, and better-articulated goals increase the acceptability of proposals made in plans. Similarly, single-purpose state mandates focus attention on natural hazards and increase the likelihood that recommendations in plans to attend to hazards will actually be acted upon. Recognizing the limits to our statistical models, these findings provide some support for the theoretical assertions put forward in chapter 1 that stronger state mandates and higher-quality local plans help foster stronger implementation of plan recommendations.

The Development Management Program

We turn now to local governmental use of different development management techniques and strategies. This analysis examines the factors that lead local governments to adopt and implement more, or different, techniques and strategies, whether or not they are proposed in a comprehensive plan. While recognizing that certain techniques may be more useful than others, we assume that more-effective hazard mitigation will occur when govern-

2. The adjusted coefficient of determination is .21 ($F = 2.76$, $p < .01$, $N = 92$). Standardized regression coefficients are: state planning mandate dummy variable, $-.06$ ($p > .05$); state single-purpose mandate strength, .20 ($p > .05$); plan quality, .25 ($p > .05$); number of policy recommendations made in plan, $-.34$ ($p < .05$); political demands for solutions, .22 ($p < .05$); planning staff commitment to hazard mitigation, .04 ($p > .05$); planning staff per capita, .05 ($p > .05$); size of hazard area, $-.23$ ($p > .05$); demand for land in hazard area, .04 ($p > .05$); catastrophic losses since 1990, $-.05$ ($p > .05$); 1990 population, .15 ($p > .05$); population growth from 1980 to 1990, .10 ($p > .05$); wealth, .001 ($p > .05$); and population density, $-.25$ ($p < .05$).

ments use more, and more varied, techniques and strategies for reducing potential losses from natural hazards.

Local governments are using a number of different strategies in managing development to reduce hazards. Employment of building standards and site design requirements is most common, with over 80 percent of local governments adopting each approach. Three-quarters of these employ structural protection to control hazards, and between 60 and 70 percent use land use controls and programs to increase public awareness of hazards and understanding of self-protective measures that can be taken to reduce losses. Even the least commonly used strategy, measures to protect public facilities and infrastructure, is used by over half of the jurisdictions.

Local governments with land use plans use more development management techniques than local governments without plans (on average, 8.6 versus 6.1 techniques). As important, those with plans employ a different mix of techniques as well. Governments with plans, on average, use twice the number of land use controls and site design requirements as governments without plans (1.1 versus 0.6 land use control measures and 1.8 versus 0.9 site design requirements). The use of more of these techniques by governments with plans shows the ability of plans to guide the location and nature of land development before it occurs. In addition, however, governments with plans are also more likely to be using measures for structural hazard control, which have been adopted in greater number than either land use or site design measures. This is important because it indicates that plans help communities develop balanced programs of hazard mitigation that use a full range of mitigation techniques.

Local governments with and without plans use about the same number of building standard and knowledge enhancement techniques. This equivalence reflects the pervasive influence of the National Flood Insurance Program, which uses building standards and floodplain mapping (a knowledge enhancement technique) to control flood losses so that insurance remains affordable.

Another way of looking at the effects of plans on the choice of hazard itigation strategies is to hold the number of hazard mitigation techniques used constant and compare the relative proportion of techniques that comprise a local government's hazard mitigation program. This approach leads to the same conclusions as when the absolute number of techniques is compared. As shown in figure 8.2; the development management programs of governments with plans include a higher proportion of land use controls and site design requirements than the programs of governments without plans. Governments without plans rely more heavily on building standards and

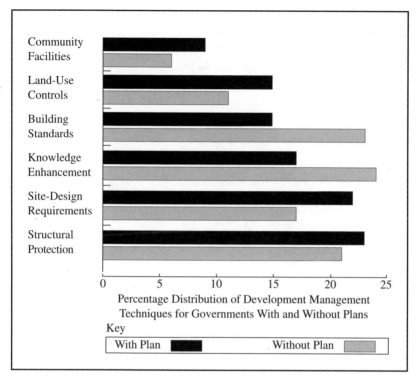

FIGURE 8.2 Plans and Development Management

knowledge enhancement techniques. Local governments with and without plans use an equivalent proportion of structural measures controlling hazards in their hazard mitigation programs (although, as noted above, governments with plans use twice the absolute number of different types of structural controls).

Factors Affecting the Strength of Development Management Programs

The analyses in chapter 7 demonstrate that plans in states with comprehensive-planning mandates address hazard management goals more thoroughly than plans in states without such mandates. Here, we focus on how plans, planning agency commitment and capacity, and other factors affect local governmental use of development management techniques. We theorized in chapter 1 that the strength of state mandates and the quality of local plans

have an effect on the adoption and use of development management techniques. As further discussed in chapter 7, governments with higher-quality
plans should be expected to adopt more complete development management programs for hazard mitigation. To test these notions, we conducted a
series of multivariate analyses of local development management programs.[3]
In what follows, we explain the effects of state mandates, the quality of local

3. For the total number of development management techniques adopted, the adjusted coefficient of determination is .43 ($F = 12.76, p < .0001, N = 172$). Standardized
regression coefficients are: state single-purpose mandate strength, .14 ($p < .05$); plan
quality, .11 ($p < .05$); planning staff commitment to hazard mitigation, .23 ($p < .001$);
elected official commitment to hazard mitigation, .12 ($p < .05$); political demands for solutions, .27 ($p < .001$); size of hazard area, $-.09$ ($p > .05$); demand for land in hazard
area, .33 ($p < .001$); catastrophic losses since 1970, .03 ($p > .05$); population density,
$-.10$ ($p > .05$); wealth, $-.04$ ($p > .05$); and planning staff per capita, .02 ($p > .05$).
We also conducted regression analyses for each development management strategy.
The results are as follows:
Land use controls. The adjusted coefficient of determination is .30, ($F = 7.63, p <
.001, N = 172$). Standardized regression coefficients are: state single-purpose mandate
strength, .24 ($p < .001$); plan quality, .23 ($p < .001$); planning staff commitment to hazard
mitigation, .07 ($p > .05$); elected official commitment to hazard mitigation, .07 ($p > .05$);
political demands for solutions, .17 ($p < .05$); size of hazard area, $-.19$ ($p < .01$); demand
for land in hazard area, .20 ($p < .05$); catastrophic losses since 1970, .03 ($p > .05$); population density, $-.16$ ($p < .05$); wealth, $-.05$ ($p > .05$); and planning staff per capita, .09
($p > .05$).
Site design standards. The adjusted coefficient of determination is .34, ($F = 9.06, p <
.001, N = 172$). Standardized regression coefficients are: state single-purpose mandate
strength, .23 ($p < .001$); plan quality, .10 ($p > .05$); planning staff commitment to hazard
mitigation, .18 ($p < .01$); elected official commitment to hazard mitigation, .08 ($p > .05$);
political demands for solutions, .13 ($p < .05$); size of hazard area, $-.19$ ($p < .01$); demand
for land in hazard area, .34 ($p < .001$); catastrophic losses since 1970, $-.15$ ($p < .05$);
1990 population density, $-.12$ ($p > .05$); wealth, $-.02$ ($p > .05$); and planning staff per
capita, .04 ($p > .05$).
Building standards. The adjusted coefficient of determination is .16, ($F = 3.98, p <
.001, N = 172$). Standardized regression coefficients are: state single-purpose mandate
strength, .10 ($p > .05$); plan quality, .12 ($p > .05$); planning staff commitment to hazard
mitigation, .11 ($p > .05$); elected official commitment to hazard mitigation, .06 ($p > .05$);
political demands for solutions, .21 ($p < .01$); size of hazard area, .17 ($p < .05$); demand
for land in hazard area, .13 ($p > .05$); catastrophic losses since 1970, $-.01$ ($p > .05$);
population density, $-.11$ ($p < .05$); wealth, $-.06$ ($p > .05$); and planning staff per capita,
$-.07$ ($p > .05$).
Knowledge enhancement techniques. The adjusted coefficient of determination is .37,
($F = 10.17, p < .001, N = 172$). Standardized regression coefficients are: state single-
purpose mandate strength, $-.26$ ($p < .001$); plan quality, .05 ($p > .05$); planning staff
commitment to hazard mitigation, .32 ($p < .001$); elected official commitment to hazard
mitigation, .06 ($p > .05$); political demands for solutions, .34 ($p < .001$); size of hazard
area, .17 ($p < .01$); demand for land in hazard area, .20 ($p < .01$); catastrophic losses since

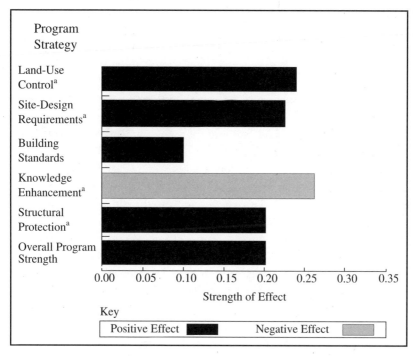

FIGURE 8.3 Effects of State Single-Purpose Mandate on Program Strategies
[a] Effect statistically significant ($p < .05$).

comprehensive plans, and other factors on the overall strength of develop-ment management programs and on the use of specific types of manage-ment techniques.

The Influence of State Mandates

Single-purpose mandates have a strong stimulating effect on the use of most development management techniques to mitigate losses from natural haz-ards, as shown in figure 8.3. They tend to foster the use of land use controls,

1970, .17 ($p < .01$); population density, .13 ($p < .05$); wealth, $-.10$ ($p > .05$); and plan-ning staff per capita, $-.02$ ($p > .05$).

Structural protection. The adjusted coefficient of determination is .17 ($F = 4.63$, $p < .001$, $N = 172$). Standardized regression coefficients are: state single-purpose mandate strength, .20 ($p < .01$); plan quality, $-.07$ ($p > .05$); planning staff commitment to hazard mitigation, .29 ($p < .001$); political demands for solutions, .29 ($p < .001$); size of hazard area, .05 ($p > .05$); demand for land in hazard area, .08 ($p > .05$); catastrophic losses since 1970, $-.01$ ($p > .05$); population density, $-.11$ ($p > .05$); wealth, .05 ($p > .05$); and plan-ning staff per capita, $-.09$ ($p > .05$).

site design standards, and structural protection; but they are associated with the use of fewer knowledge enhancement techniques. They have little association with the use of building standards.

The positive effects on local government use of land use controls and site design standards can be attributed to several notable state single-purpose mandates, described in chapters 2 through 5, that foster these approaches. These mandates include the following: in California, the Alquist-Priola Special Studies Zones Act, which requires local governments to restrict development of fault zones; the California Environmental Quality Act, which requires local governments and developers to mitigate adverse effects revealed by environmental assessments of proposed development projects; and the California Coastal Plan, which requires efforts to preserve sensitive environments; in Florida, the Environmental Land and Water Management Act, which requires special efforts to protect selected areas of critical state concern; and the Beach and Shoreline Preservation Act, which can be used to prevent development in areas of accelerated erosion; and in Washington, the Shoreline Management Act, which requires local governments to regulate land use within two hundred feet of the shorelines of ocean beaches, Puget Sound, and the Straits of San Juan de Fuca. Our data show that these focused state efforts have a marked impact on local hazard mitigation programs, pushing local governments to use land use and site design strategies. A number of states also have programs that ease the use of structural measures for control of hazards by local governments. Noteworthy programs in this regard include legislation in California, Florida, and Texas that creates or fosters creation of regional and local flood control districts and legislation in Florida that eases the use of measures fostering structural protection of beaches.

In contrast with these state programs, the efforts of the states to use single-purpose mandates to create more public information about natural hazards and to foster local use of building standards have little discernible impact. There are two reasons for this. First, information about natural hazards provided by federal programs, such as the National Flood Insurance Program and the hazard mapping efforts of the U.S. Geological Survey, may overwhelm the much more modest efforts of state governments. That may also be true for building code standards. Although each of the states except Texas has a state building code agency, as shown earlier in table 6.2, none of these programs is well financed. The largest expenditure for hazard mitigation per affected local jurisdiction is made by the state of North Carolina, and it is just twenty-five hundred dollars, not an amount that is likely to have much effect on the attention local governments give to natural hazards in their own code enforcement efforts. Second, although Texas has few single-purpose mandates, local governments there employ a number of information strategies. That provides another explanation for the negative association of single-purpose mandates with the use of information measures to deal with natural hazards.

Plan Quality

The analysis presented earlier in this chapter indicated that higher-quality plans are more likely to be implemented than lower-quality plans. Our statistical analysis shows that the overall quality of plans has a positive, but relatively small, impact on the total number of development management techniques local governments use (see figure 8.4). The relatively limited effect of plans probably stems from the puny nature of most plans, which on average make relatively few proposals for managing development to reduce losses from hazards. In addition, the plans we reviewed as the most current ones in use were generally more than five years old, with an average adoption date of 1983. Linda Dalton (1989) has reported that local governments tend to follow recent plans more closely than those that are out of date. Interviews with local planners brought to light that many of the older plans were not developed by the same staff or approved by the same group of elected officials who had adopted the current development management techniques. To deal with this problem, states with stronger planning mandates, such as Florida and North Carolina, require that plans be updated every five to seven years. The weaker California mandate merely recommends that plans be updated regularly, and the states without mandates leave updates of plans wholly to the discretion of local governments.

In addition to deficiencies in the plans in place in communities, there are several other reasons why plans do not have a stronger effect. For example, the apparent weakness of planning may simply reflect the fact that governments rely on a variety of sources of input for the particular mix of policies they pursue. We are also well aware of local planning history in which zoning and other implementing ordinances have preceded, or been substituted for, plans (see Black 1968). The institutional structure of local government may play a role as well (see Bryson 1978). Typically, planning staff are organized into long-range or advance-planning sections that draft plans, while current planning sections administer the development management program. Separate departments, such as emergency management or public works, may be in charge of addressing natural hazards. (Planning departments were the lead agency for dealing with hazards in only 18 percent of the local govern-

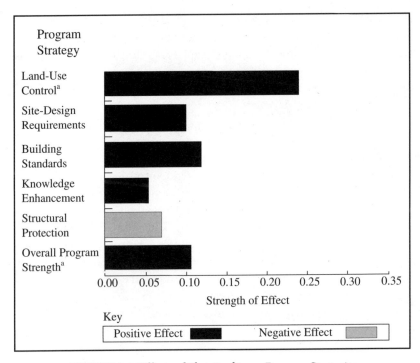

FIGURE 8.4 Effects of Plan Quality on Program Strategies
[a] Effect statistically significant ($p < .05$).

ments studied.) Thus, despite arguments and legislation favoring consistency between a local plan and development management, the involvement of different personnel inevitably leads to differences in approach and detail.

When we looked at the use of specific development management strategies, we also found that plans have little stimulating effect, with one exception. The exception is noteworthy, however, in that we find comprehensive plans promote the adoption of land use strategies for dealing with hazards. Because such strategies have been particularly difficult to put in place in local government, state planning mandates may represent one of the few avenues state and federal policy makers have for accomplishing this policy end.

Although with the exception of land use strategies plans have only a small direct effect on the strength of local development management programs, they have a marked indirect effect through their impacts on the commitment of planning staff to hazard mitigation and their ability to energize a

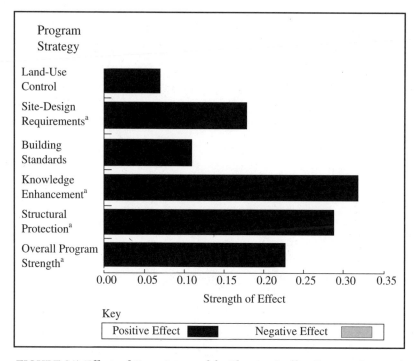

FIGURE 8.5 Effects of Commitment of the Planning Staff on Program Strategies
[a] Effect statistically significant ($p < .05$).

political constituency for mitigation (these effects of plans are discussed in chapter 7). Both staff commitment and political demands have a strong positive effect on the strength of local development management programs.

Planning Agency Commitment

The commitment of planning agencies proves to be one of the most important predictors of the use of development management techniques for hazard mitigation. When the staff is committed to doing something about natural hazards, local governments tend to put in place a larger array of development management techniques, as illustrated in figure 8.5. Our analyses indicate that the commitment of elected officials is less important than that of staff in fostering stronger development management programs. The technical nature of many development management techniques for dealing with hazards may require that the impetus for adoption come from the planning staff rather than from elected officials. We found that staff capacity is not associated with the number of development management measures adopted. Thus, to paraphrase the observation of policy analysts William Petak and Arthur Atkisson (1982) quoted in the preceding chapter, the key to more effective mitigation programs in local governments truly is the willingness of planners to act rather than local agencies' capacity to do something about hazards.

Constituency Demands

As with their influence on commitment (see chapter 7) and on plan implementation (noted earlier in this chapter), political demands for action strongly affect the strength of development management programs. The more active interest groups have been in demanding attention to natural hazards, the more hazard mitigation techniques local governments have adopted (see figure 8.6). Among business, environmental, and neighborhood groups, policy demands from environmental groups have the strongest effect on the strength of the overall development management program and on the pursuit of land use and knowledge enhancement strategies.[4] As noted in the previous chapter, the information contained in land use plans empowers environmental and neighborhood groups, which are twice as likely to demand attention to hazards in communities with plans as in communities without plans. Demands by business groups have the strongest effect on the use of structural protection measures, and demands by business and neighborhood groups have a strong effect on the use of both building and site design standards to mitigate hazards.

4. The same specifications of regression models reported in note 3 above were employed, but instead of the overall political demand index, we substituted measures of demands from business groups, environmental groups, and neighborhood groups. Demands from each group tended to stimulate local government adoption of hazard mitigation techniques. The standardized regression coefficients for each group with the overall strength of the development management program are: business groups, .30; environmental groups, .37; neighborhood groups, .31; with the use of land use control techniques: business groups, .15; environmental groups, .20; neighborhood groups, .17; with the use of knowledge enhancement techniques: business groups, .31; environmental groups, .35; neighborhood groups, .29; with the use of building and site design standards: business groups, .20; environmental groups, .15; neighborhood groups, .20; with the use of structural protection techniques: business groups, .17; environmental groups, .14; neighborhood groups, .08; and with the use of community facility design and location techniques: business groups, .15; environmental groups, .23; neighborhood groups, .21.

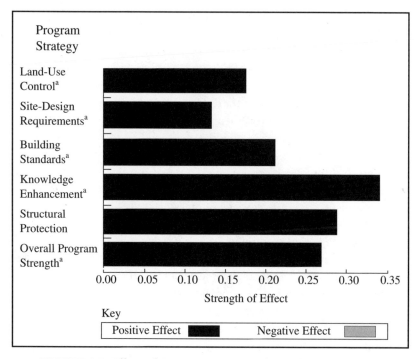

FIGURE 8.6 Effects of Constituency Demands on Program Strategies

[a] Effect statistically significant ($p < .05$).

Other Situational Factors

The demand for land in areas subject to natural hazards, which we believed would make mitigation less tractable, is positively associated with the number of hazard mitigation techniques adopted. Development pressures on hazardous areas signal the need for hazard reduction measures, and local governments heed that signal, even though it also suppresses commitment. Among the other situational factors we examined (staff capacity, wealth, size of the hazard zone, previous occurrence of a natural disaster, population density), none has a strong effect on the number of mitigation techniques employed. In the case of the specific strategies employed for hazard mitigation, land use controls are less likely to be used when population densities are high and when a larger proportion of a community is located in areas subject to hazards. Obviously, in these cases land use controls are likely to stifle economic growth, and therefore they are the least appropriate of the strategies governments might use.

Plans and Planning Agency Commitment

We found that plans and planners' commitment interact to shape the character of development management programs. When local governments lack both plans and committed planners, they tend to rely heavily on building standards to deal with natural hazards. That probably reflects the impact of other mandates on local governments. The National Flood Insurance Program, for example, emphasizes building elevation to mitigate flood hazards, as do state building code requirements, which establish minimum standards to be enforced by local governments in four of the five states we studied (California, Florida, North Carolina, and Washington). With more commitment from planners, in the absence of high-quality plans governments add measures to increase public information, but they tend to avoid land use controls and site design requirements.

With a plan, but with little commitment to hazard mitigation, communities tend to rely more heavily on land use controls to manage development. As commitment increases, governments with plans tend to pursue programs that employ a more balanced mix of available hazard mitigation techniques. Thus, plans tend to steer communities away from sole dependence on building standards and knowledge enhancement techniques and toward land use controls and site design requirements. The commitment of planners to hazard reduction is less important in the use of these land use and site-planning techniques. Indeed, the more anticipatory or preventive approach relying on land use controls clearly depends more on the existence of a good plan than on a high level of agency commitment, whereas the less interventionist informational approach depends on a planning agency strongly committed to addressing hazards in the absence of a plan. With both a plan and commitment, communities use both land use and information techniques.

Summary And Conclusions

The theoretical framework we developed in chapter 1 suggested that states could improve local development management programs if they could improve the quality of local comprehensive plans, increase the commitment of local officials to address planning issues, and foster plan implementation. The analyses of this chapter confirm the importance of these factors.

Our findings suggest that development management is qualitatively different in communities with plans. That is, the nature of development management changes when mandates and plans (especially good-quality ones) are present. Plans stimulate local government adoption of land use strategies for dealing with hazards and, when planners also become committed to hazard mitigation, a balanced mix of strategies that includes both land use techniques and other approaches to mitigation.

The findings we have reviewed raise three issues for policy makers. First, given the attention by states and localities to plan making, how can (or how should) the influence of local plans be expanded beyond their current important but limited role, to encompass and coordinate all aspects of managing development? Without such expansion, the production of plans will continue to appear too focused on land use issues, or as more an end in itself than a means for improving municipal development management.

Second, given the importance of local factors that the state cannot control (such as local environmental conditions and growth pressures), how can (or how should) state actions enhance the commitment of the local planning agency to state policy objectives? Despite relatively strong differences in the features of state planning mandates and in the effort employed, the commitment of local planning agencies to state policy goals varies only slightly with the strength of the planning mandate. The influence on commitment of state mandates and the plans they foster is indirect. Mandates and plans build commitment through enhancement of stakeholder knowledge of hazards and the political demands such knowledge stimulates. Our findings suggest that the current state attempts to build commitment to specific policy goals through such planning mandate features as awareness building, funding, and sanctions, or to increase capacity by providing information and technical assistance, are not getting through to local planning agencies. These measures help produce better plans (and through plans indirectly enhance commitment to state goals) but have no direct effects on commitment. Because local commitment is critical to pursuit of a strong, balanced development management program, finding ways to affect it more directly is an important task.

Third, our finding that single-purpose mandates have affected the strength of local development management programs raises this question: How can (or how should) states apply the strengths of both planning and single-purpose mandates to achieve state policy objectives? Our findings provide evidence that both state approaches are needed if states are to affect local government policy in ways that achieve state objectives. State planning mandates help with building a political constituency for hazard mitigation and also with placing land use controls and site design requirements on the table, but they may be too broad to directly affect commitment to specific policy objectives. The single-purpose mandates are also needed to foster attention to the specific problems with which the state is grappling. Single-purpose mandates also augment plans in fostering land use approaches to the accomplishment of hazard mitigation and, by implication, other state goals.

The policy recommendations made by local comprehensive plans tend to be implemented. Plans contribute to stronger development management programs and to programs that apply land use solutions to policy problems. Even more can be accomplished, however, if mandates and plans have a stronger impact on the commitment of local planners to state policy goals. Finding ways to do that poses a number of important questions for state (and federal) policy makers.

III

Prospects for Making
Governments Plan

9

Rethinking Planning Mandates

Evaluations of state comprehensive-planning mandates that were adopted in the 1970s noted their good intentions while highlighting their complexity and apparent ineffectiveness in improving development management. The consensus seemed to be that they might work in some smaller states, like Hawaii or Vermont, but the conflicts over land use in larger states were too complicated and resources too limited for a comprehensive-planning solution. Instead, many states opted to adopt single-purpose mandates that addressed pressing environmental issues while minimizing conflicts over the appropriate use of land.

Concerns about limitations of single-purpose mandates along with new growth pressures in the mid-1980s fueled for a number of states a new set of state comprehensive-planning mandates that focus on the management of growth. This new set of planning mandates attended to some of the deficiencies of earlier planning approaches. Their policy designs incorporate key tenets of planning and implementation theory in emphasizing such things as state and local collaboration, vertical (top-down) and horizontal (interlocal) consistency, and state efforts to increase local capacity for planning. Yet the newer planning mandates retain if not increase the complexity of objectives that were the nemesis of the earlier planning mandates.

Many promising features have been highlighted in the dozens of articles and several books describing individual state efforts and comparing programs across states. But that promise has not been systematically evaluated. What follows is a summary of our assessment of state comprehensive-planning mandates and the implications of our study for theorizing and policy.

Assessing Comprehensive-Planning Mandates

This book has addressed the influence of state comprehensive-planning mandates upon local land use planning and development management actions. In theorizing about the potential effects of state planning mandates, we identified two linchpins. One is the design of the state mandate. This consists of the planning requirements of the mandates and features aimed at enhancing the commitment of local governments to state goals and their capacity to carry out planning and development management. We reason that these provisions of mandates signal state objectives and set expectations about local government performance. As such, the mandate design structures implementation at state and local levels. The second key linchpin is the local plan. Plans are the key target, but not the exclusive target, of comprehensive-planning mandates. Failure to enhance the number, quality, or character of local plans would constitute direct evidence that planning mandates are ineffective.

Plans are not ends in themselves. The newer planning mandates use local and regional plans as a vehicle for fostering and coordinating local growth management. Our particular focus is the extent to which these mandates and resultant plans enhance local management of development in hazard-prone areas. The existence of other, single-purpose environmental mandates for addressing these goals in most states leads to a questioning of the necessity of state comprehensive-planning mandates and local plans. At issue is what is gained in achieving state goals by adding a layer of planning mandates that is not accomplished by the single-purpose mandates. This leads us to consider the way in which plans, in response to planning mandates, affect development management.

By comparing the experience of local governments in states (and state subareas) with and without comprehensive-planning mandates, we have been able to empirically evaluate the influence of mandates on local plans and the influence of mandates and plans on local development management. Four key findings emerge from our analyses. First, state planning mandates strongly affect the quality and character of local plans. Second, the design of the mandates and related implementation styles of state agencies shape the extent and character of state policy influence. Third, the existence and quality of local plans, along with the commitment of local officials to state policy goals, influence the character and effort going into local development management. Fourth, beyond their key influence on the quality of plans, the planning mandates that we consider have relatively little influence upon other factors that affect the success of local planning and development management.

The first three findings provide a positive endorsement of key elements of the new generation of comprehensive-planning mandates. We provide a much more hopeful picture than that provided by assessments of the first generation of mandates. We have shown that state planning mandates can foster local attention to solutions that may not be addressed under single-purpose environmental regulations. The fourth finding is more pessimistic. Although planning mandates make a difference, that difference is still a marginal one. This suggests much can be done to improve the influence of state planning mandates.

State Comprehensive-Planning Mandates Matter

Our findings confirm that state comprehensive-planning mandates, at least in the hazards area and by implication in other key planning areas, make a positive difference in the existence, character, and quality of local plans. It is reassuring to find that local governments are more likely to prepare comprehensive plans when required to do so. Equally important is the finding that planning mandates foster a substantial improvement in the quality of plans. For states that require comprehensive plans of local governments and follow-through on those requirements, local plans have more substantial factual underpinnings, goals tend to be stated more clearly, and local policies for guiding development are stronger.

However, a number of local governments prepare plans without a requirement to do so from state government. Our findings show that state mandates substitute for local demands to address development pressures. As a consequence, state mandates are an important impetus for developing plans. But where local demands to address development are strong and community resources high, local policy makers appear to be responsive in using plans as tools for managing development regardless of the existence of a state mandate requiring them to prepare plans. This is illustrated in our study by the frequent use of local plans in Washington state, where, at the time of our study, no comprehensive-planning mandate existed. In areas for which such demands are not as strong, illustrated in our study by Texas and the North Carolina mountains, the local planning response is much more muted. For these areas, state mandates are necessary to substitute for the lack of political demands in fostering planning solutions to growth and environmental problems. Lacking such demands and state mandates, we find infrequent use of plans in Texas and the North Carolina mountains. The few local plans in these areas are generally quite weak in comparison with those plans developed in response to state planning mandates.

These key findings about the influence of comprehensive-planning mandates on plan quality, and those summarized below about their influence on development management, counter the arguments of those who are skeptical about state planning requirements and local government plan making (e.g., Alexander and Faludi 1989). Our findings clearly show planning mandates can make a difference in the attention local governments give to land use and development management.

State Mandate Design and Implementation Efforts Matter

It is an overgeneralization to conclude that all comprehensive-planning mandates—or even all newer forms of planning mandates—are effective. Our findings show that the influence of planning mandates varies considerably among the states under study. We also find variation in the influence of single-purpose mandates upon development management. Except for the added complexity of planning mandates, the differences in design between comprehensive-planning and single-purpose mandates are more matters of degree than sharp contrasts.

We attribute variation in mandate influence on local policy to differences in the design of mandate legislation and to differences in the strength of the efforts that relevant state agencies expend in carrying out the legislation. Our empirical models show that mandates are more effective when they contain features aimed at building local commitment to prepare plans (and, to a lesser extent, capacity), when there is a strong commitment by relevant state agencies to the goals of the legislation, and when there are strong implementation efforts by these agencies. Florida's success with its comprehensive program for growth management illustrates the importance of both policy features that build local governmental commitment and accompanying strong implementation efforts by state agencies. The success of Washington state in employing single-purpose mandates to induce local governments to pay attention to flood hazards and shoreline management illustrates the importance of these same factors for effective single-purpose mandates. These successes can be contrasted with less-effective comprehensive planning in California and less-effective single-purpose mandates in Texas. In these latter instances, the state policy designs contain few commitment- and capacity-building features, and relevant state agencies put little effort into implementing the mandates.

The details of mandate design, along with high degrees of commitment and capacity on the part of state agencies, are important in shaping the character of the day-to-day dealings between state agencies and local governments. Our findings show that it is relatively easy to bring about a formal and legalistic approach to local governments. In contrast, it is more difficult to bring about collaborative relationships that are sought with the second generation of comprehensive-planning mandates. Half-hearted attempts to bring about comprehensive planning, brought about by failing to provide state agencies with sufficient resources or tools with which to work, can backfire. These findings underscore the importance of appropriate mandate designs and committed state agencies for achieving successful outcomes.

State Planning Mandates and Local Plans Affect Development Management

Our findings reaffirm what planners have long believed but lacked evidence to substantiate: plans that are based on sound analysis of the facts, formulate clear policy goals, and set forth appropriate policy recommendations result in stronger development management. Because of the role of high-quality plans in shaping local development management, state comprehensive-planning mandates are also important. By influencing the quality and character of local plans, planning mandates in turn influence the extent and character of local development management. They do that directly by providing information and ideas for development management and indirectly by creating shared knowledge that energizes political constituencies. Shared knowledge helps to foster commitment to state policy goals among local elected officials and planning staff.

A key point about comprehensive-planning mandates is that the character of local development management changes when strong mandates come into play. We find the quality of local plans and the commitment of planning staff jointly affect the choice of development management strategies. Building standards represent the default approach and dominate the few techniques in use by communities without plans or planners committed to hazard management. Most communities in our study, characterized by varied commitment and plans of low to moderate quality, end up emphasizing a few land use controls, site design standards, or programs for knowledge enhancement. Only those communities with both strong planning commitment and good plans undertake a more balanced approach.

By enacting comprehensive-planning mandates, states can gain several things that they cannot accomplish as well by enacting single-purpose mandates. First, planning mandates prompt local governments to pay attention to land use and standards for site design as instruments for managing development in areas that are prone to hazards. Comprehensive-planning mandates put these tools on the table and give physical planners a stake in development regulation. Second, planning mandates provide for more balance in the approaches local governments employ in managing development by fostering use of land use controls. Third, these mandates seek greater coordination in efforts to reach different environmental management goals.

Limited Effects on Commitment

The more pessimistic findings concern the limited effect that mandates have in enhancing commitment of local officials to state goals for managing hazards and, by extension, to other aspects of development management. We thought of mandates as tools to persuade and enable local officials to embrace state policy objectives. We theorized that, with greater commitment (and capacity), local governments would develop stronger hazard management programs. However, neither the single-purpose nor the comprehensive-planning mandates in our study directly affected the commitment of local officials to state goals. We also thought that the process of developing plans would instill greater commitment to hazard management. We found evidence for this through the role of plans in enhancing knowledge and awareness of hazard problems, which in turn, help to foster constituencies for addressing the problems.

The point is that we found a much weaker influence of mandates and plan making on the commitment of local officials to state goals than expected from our theorizing. Were it merely a matter of our theory being wrong, these negative findings would be of little concern. But the findings have serious implications. One of our more consistent findings is that the commitment of local officials is a strong influence upon the extent of plan implementation and strength of development management efforts. Our statistical modeling suggests a much stronger influence would arise if mandates had a stronger impact on commitment of local officials.

Revisiting Our Theory and Data

Our theorizing about planning mandates, plans, and development management specifies the paths by which planning mandates structure and help ease local planning and development management. We theorized that comprehensive-planning mandates influence the quality of plans through specification of plan content and form. We also expected planning mandates to foster greater local commitment to state policy goals and to enhance the capacity of local governments to plan. These factors, as mediated by situational factors, are critical intermediary points in our theorizing about the influence that state mandates have on local development management.

In most respects the findings are supportive of our theorizing. Indeed, the strength of the empirical evidence for the influence of planning mandates upon plan quality is striking. This is especially true given that our data about mandate design, situational factors, and plan quality come from independent sources. The findings about mandate design and implementation are also striking in that they extend notions about intergovernmental implementation that have not been previously examined empirically. Of particular note is our evidence that statutory coherence is not a necessary condition for strong policy implementation. We show that potential implementation difficulties of complex legislation, reflected in comprehensive-planning mandates, can be compensated for by including appropriate facilitating features and by strong state agency commitment to the objectives of the legislation.

Two Areas for Revision

Two aspects of our theorizing need to be revisited. One concerns the role of the commitment and capacity of local governments. We fail to find evidence for our theorizing that state mandates and local plans are strong tools for persuading and enabling local officials to embrace state policy objectives. Local officials respond to the mandates in developing plans and hazard management programs, but there is less evidence for increased commitment to or capacity for carrying out hazard management.

In developing our theory, we debated the direction of causal influences. One argument had it that mandates enhanced commitment and capacity and that these factors in turn led to stronger plans. Another had it that the process of putting a plan together, in response to a comprehensive-planning mandate, would engender greater commitment and capacity. In either case, we expected a strongly positive relationship between the existence (and quality) of plans and the commitment and capacity of local governments. The statistical models suggest at best a weak link based on the role of plans in building a common base of knowledge and understanding. This finding leaves us in somewhat of a quandary about the theory. As noted in the preceding discussion, this also raises important policy questions.

Failure to detect a stronger relationship does not necessarily mean our theorizing is incorrect. As noted below, we think that our findings in part reflect insufficient specification of our statistical models. However, it may be that commitment and capacity are not as important intervening variables as we hypothesize. Our findings suggest that the key driver of local action is community demands. Where such demands are lacking, state mandates play an important role in stimulating local action. Where such demands are strong, local officials are responsive and undertake hazard management programs. Of interest for further research is how plans and planning stimulate community demands and how these demands translate into effective action.

A second area of theorizing that needs to be revisited concerns the relation between local comprehensive plans and development management. In our theorizing, we questioned the presumptions of the planning literature about the role of consistency requirements of state mandates. We hypothesized that only if plans were up-to-date and of high quality would such requirements help foster stronger development management. Our findings lead to a revision in this hypothesis. In particular, up-to-date and high-quality plans appear to be insufficient for fostering balanced development management programs. Such conditions, absent strong commitment, lead to limited programs that focus on land use and site design considerations. Only with the additional presence of a strong commitment to state objectives are plans effective in helping to foster development management programs that encompass a broader set of approaches, some of which are less familiar to planners.

Caveats to Our Study

Our choice to focus on natural hazards was a conscious decision aimed at providing focus to our data collection and comparability across states. As noted in chapter 1, we think there are good reasons why issues concerning natural hazards serve as a microcosm of broader debates about land use. Given the legacy of hazards management being relegated to the backwaters of local planning, one might expect no discernible effect of state comprehensive-planning or single-purpose mandates upon local management of hazards. Instead, our findings show that state mandates can induce greater attention to hazards by local governments when preparing comprehensive plans and when carrying out development management programs. Nonetheless, the effects of state mandates are modest at best.

The limited outcomes in influencing the level of commitment to and capacity for hazard management raise a question: are the mandates weakly implemented, or is hazard management an especially difficult area in which to bring about change? The evidence suggests that both are somewhat true. The effort state agencies, except in Florida, put into implementing the hazard components of the single-purpose and comprehensive-planning mandates is low (a median state expenditure in 1990, including state personnel costs, of $637 per affected local jurisdictions for all but the Florida mandates). The difficulty of bringing about change in local hazard management practices is underscored by the hazards researchers (e.g., Burby and French 1981; May and Williams 1986).

These considerations argue for replication of this study in other policy arenas with similar, systematic empirical research. As argued by John Bryson (1991), such research is essential for establishing the importance of planning as a key component of state and local policy making. Any such extensions should include better assessment of implementation by measuring the amount of state financial aid, technical assistance, and other educational efforts and by assessing the extent of state review of local plans. Such data would make it possible to assess whether mandates can be useful tools for building commitment and local capacity. Our research suggests limited impacts in these respects, but we really do not know if that is because mandates are ineffective in this regard or if the state targeting of financial and technical assistance is problematic.

It is also useful to pay greater attention to the conceptualization of commitment of local officials to higher-level policy goals. The intergovernmental implementation literature cites the importance of normative commitment that is derived from the beliefs of planners and elected officials about the soundness of state objectives. However, there are other forms of commitment that also could be important. We have not been able to distinguish these adequately. These include commitment to obey state prescriptions based on calculations of the benefits and costs of compliance (calculated compliance) and commitment based on professional relationships between state and local officials (associational commitment).

The different types of commitment are potentially important in helping to understand different ways to achieve compliance with mandates. Top-down planning programs such as Florida's growth management effort appear to be effective in fostering compliance with planning prescriptions. This probably arises from calculated commitment as local governments respond to the mandate's relatively strong coercive provisions. We hypothesize that normative commitment would not be strengthened in such circumstances. As a consequence, mandates like Florida's growth management legislation that use sanctions to bend local governments to the state's will limit their potential impact on endorsement of state policy objectives by local government officials.

A closely related topic for further investigation is the role of plans and plan making in empowering citizens to become active in demanding governmental attention to improper land use or development. This addresses the notion of communicative rationality that some planning theorists have argued is an important aspect of plan making. We were able to explore this function only in a cursory way by looking at the extent to which more serious planning processes (reflected by higher-quality plans) are associated with awareness of hazards and greater political demands to address problems. Advancing an understanding of this aspect of plan making requires a more systematic assessment of these relationships.

Future studies should also pay greater attention to implementation over time. Having good measures prior to and after mandates come into effect or major changes are made makes it much easier to separate out their effects from those of other factors. For example, it would be possible to assess the hypothesis that preparation of plans influences commitment and capacity if data about these factors were available for the periods prior to and after completion of plans. Lacking such data over time, we have relied upon comparisons of local governments with and without plans along with appropriate statistical controls.

Policy Implications

The overall message of this book is clear: state comprehensive-planning mandates make a difference. The policy implication is that states that ignore comprehensive-planning mandates are forsaking an important policy tool for addressing development management issues. However, the influence of such mandates rests on the particulars of policy design and implementation. What follows are the implications we draw about federal policy, state choices about mandates, state mandate design and implementation, and the improvement of the quality of local plans as a basis for guiding development management.

Implications for Federal Hazards Policies

The reluctance of federal policy makers to intervene in local land use decision making has resulted in states becoming the focal point for such decisions. Nonetheless, the federal government has a strong stake in local development management decisions, particularly as they affect development in hazardous areas. Two sets of implications for federal hazards policies follow.

One implication concerns those programs for which states have a central role in defining and carrying out hazard management programs. These include programs for coastal management, hurricane preparedness, and reduction of earthquake risk. Federal policy for programs should strongly encourage, if not require, states to make use of planning mandates as a tool for addressing development in hazardous areas. At present only the federal Coastal Zone Management Program makes state and local planning an important program component.

A second implication for federal hazards policies concerns those programs for which the government has attempted to influence local mitigation of hazards. The main example of this is the National Flood Insurance Program, which uses eligibility requirements for federal flood insurance to promote local governmental regulation of construction in flood-prone areas. The Federal Insurance Administration is authorized to require local plans as a condition for community participation in the flood insurance program, but it has failed to use that authorization. Our findings provide a strong case for invoking that authority.

State Mandate Choices: Mandates as Complements Rather Than Substitutes

Although federal land use planning mandates were seriously considered in the 1970s, we doubt that such intervention will be contemplated again in our lifetimes. The variation in circumstances among states and distrust of governmental intervention are too strong. As the state experiences in this study show, there are plenty of reasons for us to believe that states will continue to innovate in this important policy arena. This leads us to focus our policy discussion on the states.

State comprehensive-planning mandates can be useful tools in influencing the way that local governments address a state's objectives for development or environmental management. Although this book shows that comprehensive-planning mandates are highly desirable tools, they are by no means essential tools. The Washington state experience suggests that well-crafted single-purpose mandates, accompanied by strong state implementation efforts, can be effective in stimulating local governmental attention to particular environmental (or other) objectives.

In the introductory chapter, we outlined a number of reasons drawn from the planning literature why scholars think states should adopt comprehensive-planning mandates. Many of these benefits are difficult to assess (see Bollens 1993; Knaap 1992; Talen 1996). This book makes two key arguments in favor of adopting planning mandates. One is that comprehensive-planning mandates push local governments to use new approaches in addressing development management issues. By empowering planners and putting land use tools on the table, the mandates shift the policy mix. In the case of natural hazards, comprehensive-planning mandates draw attention away from limiting harm (i.e., through structural works and building codes) toward preventing harm through management of land use. We suspect planning mandates have similar effects for arenas other than hazards.

A second argument is that the comprehensive-planning mandates foster a much stronger store of knowledge about local problems and solutions than any single-purpose mandate can. This is reflected in the improved quality of plans in jurisdictions subject to planning mandates. Our evidence suggests that higher-quality plans help build local constituencies for state policy aims and, in turn, foster better development management programs. But perhaps as important are the less tangible aspects that some planning scholars (Faludi 1987; Sager 1990) point to in arguing that this store of knowledge provides the ingredients for policy learning and for better policy decisions.

We do not think that the choice should be framed as one between comprehensive-planning and single-purpose mandates, although we are hampered in this assessment because no states have only the former. Our findings suggest that both types of mandates are necessary if states want to encourage local support of state policy objectives. Comprehensive-planning mandates help with coordination and place standards for land use and requirements for site design on the table. But because of their breadth, they may not be as effective in enhancing commitment to specific objectives. This seems especially true when the objectives are low on local governmental agendas. Single-purpose mandates can be effective in reinforcing these objectives. As a consequence, comprehensive-planning and single-purpose mandates have the potential to effectively complement each other.

Mandate Design: Designing and Implementing Better Mandates

The challenge in designing and implementing mandates is to overcome complexity brought about by multiple goals, several layers of government, and conflicting desires among the agencies and governments responsible for carrying out the legislation. These factors undermined the effectiveness of the earlier forms of comprehensive-planning mandates. Our findings show that policy makers can overcome these problems by designing planning mandates that incorporate key design features and by strengthening the effort that goes into implementing the mandates.

One of the central aims of the newer comprehensive-planning mandates is to bring about greater state and local collaboration in achieving state goals. Under the collaborative approach, states set policy goals and objectives but leave, to varying degrees, the specific details of plan content and implementation to the discretion of local governments. This book shows that bringing about such collaboration—not only in words but in the day-to-day dealings with local governments—is not an easy undertaking.

Half-hearted comprehensive-planning legislation creates several potential dangers. One danger is that the legislation may prove to be ineffectual, in that a process is established but the tools and ability to carry it out are not there. This is the experience of many of the first wave of state comprehensive-planning mandates. A second danger arises when the mandate is taken seriously but the goals are not sufficiently reinforced through the day-to-day dealings of state agencies with local governments. Plans are developed, but they are of an uneven quality. This seems to be the experience with California's comprehensive-planning mandate. A third danger is that the philosophy of the mandate gets lost in translation, leading to a coercive policy rather than a collaborative policy. When this happens, local governmental compliance with the process and legal formalism become substitutes for collaboration and the achievement of desirable outcomes. Florida seems to have erred in this direction in implementing comprehensive-planning legislation after new provisions were added in the mid-1980s, and as a consequence it has had to cope with backlash from local governments over undesirable state actions.

Three mandate design ingredients appear to be essential for avoiding these dangers. One is adequate authority provided by the planning mandate for state agencies to monitor and enforce prescriptions about plan content (e.g., consistency provisions) and process provisions (e.g., deadlines for plan preparation). These are the teeth that many comprehensive-planning mandates lack. These provisions, when adequately implemented, stimulate local governmental actions in part because of agencies' fear of sanctions if they do not comply with mandate prescriptions.

A second ingredient is features that build normative commitment to state policy objectives. This commitment is evidenced by agreement of state and local officials about the seriousness of problems and the need for governmental intervention. We believe normative commitment is much more difficult to bring about than calculated commitment. The latter form of commitment is likely to be fleeting, in that as soon as state agencies become less vigilant, local attention to the state goals diminishes.

A third ingredient is the tools within mandates for building the capacity of local governments to carry out policies. Provisions such as technical assistance, workshops, model plan provisions, and map production, for example, are important tools for increasing capacity. These are also potentially important tools for helping to bring about normative commitment, in that such knowledge can be a basis for agreement about problems and the need for governmental intervention.

Commitment- and capacity-building tools can work to reinforce each other. The coercive teeth of mandates help to induce local governmental action. Capacity-building activities, such as workshops and technical assistance, influence normative commitment of local governments and also increase their ability to carry out the policy. The correct balance between these provisions depends on existing local capacity and commitment. Our sense is that there is often a presumption of greater local commitment to state goals than is the case. As a consequence, mandates lack sufficient provisions aimed first at inducing local actions and second at building normative commitment to policy objectives.

A well-designed mandate will be half-hearted at best if it is not backed by strong implementation efforts. This book underscores the important role that state agencies have in translating state mandate intentions into day-to-day realities. Lack of consistent and effective translation appears to be a major shortcoming of many of the mandates we studied. Finding or creating a state agency with strong commitment to the policy goals is important. Agency personnel must believe that planning (or other) objectives are to be taken seriously. Yet commitment alone is insufficient to bring about the collaborative philosophy. Sufficient state agency capacity—knowledgeable staff, funding, and technical bases—must exist for the agency to be credible as a resource in dealing with local officials. We have shown that high levels of state agency commitment without commensurate capacity only leads to legal formalism as a substitute for collaboration.

One of the more salient lessons of this book is the difficulty of bringing about collaboration, especially when there is state and local conflict over policy objectives. Collaboration cannot be legislated or purchased. The fact that there are few good models of workable collaborative planning arrangements in the United States—Florida's experience perhaps being the best to offer—makes it clear that there are noteworthy challenges.

Dealing with Variation in Local Circumstances: Targeting Provisions

Local jurisdictions vary in the extent to which they are affected by problems related to inappropriate land use. One of the appeals of comprehensive-planning approaches is that, in theory at least, they permit local responsiveness to different circumstances while also promoting state policy objectives. Yet, as we show, the willingness and ability of local governments to undertake programs to achieve state policy goals are strongly influenced by the extent of local political demands and by available community resources. Because jurisdictions differ in these respects, there is a much more uneven response by local governments to state mandates than is desired. We documented this variation for states with comprehensive-planning mandates with respect to the quality of plan provisions and the extent of development management efforts.

Given these gaps in states with planning mandates, the challenge for policy redesign is to address the needs of lagging jurisdictions. One approach is to increase the coercive features of state planning mandates in order to force reluctant local governments to comply with state desires. This, however, may lead to reluctant compliance marked by token adherence to planning provisions. Perhaps a different route is required. We think much can be accomplished if state program administrators take into greater account the needs of lagging jurisdictions when allocating planning grants and other resources. Funding for demonstration programs could be targeted toward lagging jurisdictions, so as to increase their planning and development management capabilities. This includes better targeting of technical assistance and working more closely with public officials to increase their commitment to state goals. Without such targeting, the lagging jurisdictions are likely to fall further behind.

The point is that there is almost as much variation within states as between states in planning quality and development management efforts—even with the existence of strong state planning mandates. This variation is evidenced by the relatively low explanatory power of some of our empirical models. The variation within states is a difficult challenge that has not been well addressed in the state programs we have studied.

Improving Development Management: Better-Quality Plans

One of the clear implications of this book is that local development management can be improved by both increasing the quality of local plans and enhancing the commitment of local officials to state objectives. Well-designed and well-implemented state planning mandates can result in improved plan quality. This, in turn, helps to improve attention in development management to land use and site design considerations.

Our failure to find a stronger link between recommendations contained in plans and the development management measures adopted by local governments is of concern. Managing development, not paper plans, is the ultimate objective of state planning programs. To strengthen the link, states first need to foster better local plans. We find that local plans, when prepared, tend to be implemented. But because of their anemic nature they have relatively little impact on the local governments' programs for development management. A second step is greater adoption and enforcement of state requirements for consistency between local plans and development management provisions. This could be facilitated by states providing incentives for the updating of development management provisions as local plans are revised.

Increasing commitment of local governmental officials and planners to state policy objectives is an important aspect of improving both plan quality and development management. This turns out to be a rather illusive goal, since, as our data show, the requirements of state mandates have little influence on commitment. We find that local political demands to address problems posed by development are keys to fostering such commitment. Given this, the issue is what can state (and federal) policy makers do to create such demands? We think one direction is to emphasize constituency building as an important aspect of local planning requirements. This normally entails participatory processes that involve contributions from affected stakeholders. In addition, planners might pay particular attention to professional groups—architects, engineers, real estate agents—that, for some issues, have a stronger stake in policy outcomes, are easier to reach, and are more capable of mobilizing efforts to influence state and local policy making (see May 1991).

Final Words

In this book we have attempted to assess whether state comprehensive-planning mandates have had any real impact on land use policy and management at the local level of government. This has involved a detailed look at the design and influence of state comprehensive-planning mandates in a variety of states. The questions we have raised and our approach in addressing them have been guided by theorizing, for which we have drawn on relevant literature in planning, regulatory federalism, and intergovernmental implementation. Apart from the substantive findings, we think that the book makes a noteworthy contribution in demonstrating the value of systematic, empirical study for testing and extending planning theory.

Our positive assessment of the newer forms of state comprehensive-planning mandates should be reassuring to those who have labored to design and implement such policies and to planning scholars who have thought hard about ways to improve them. Yet the message of this book is one of cautious optimism. New challenges to planning are coming forth from those concerned about property rights. These have caused some state legislatures to be reluctant to create or strengthen comprehensive-planning requirements. We do not think that such challenges necessitate a dismantling of these requirements. Instead, they require stronger justification for governmental actions and more (rather than less) attention to the details of the design of state mandates. Such rethinking leaves opportunities for considering the types of improvements in policy design that we have discussed in this book.

Appendix

Research Design and Measurement of Variables

This study is based on a systematic comparative research design, in which planning for hazard mitigation under state comprehensive-planning and single-purpose mandates is compared, at both state and local government levels, to planning where there are no such mandates.

At the local governmental level, the study focuses on a random sample of 176 municipalities and counties in five states. Eighty-eight of those communities are in three states (California, Florida, and the coastal zone of North Carolina) with comprehensive-planning mandates. Another sample comprises eighty-eight communities from Texas, Washington, and the mountain region of North Carolina that are not subject to a state mandate to have a comprehensive plan. The eighty-eight communities subject to planning mandates are compared to the eighty-eight communities not subject to planning mandates to explore two research questions: Does state-mandated comprehensive planning make a difference in the quality of local government planning? Does state-mandated planning make a difference in local government management of development?

The 176 communities can also be divided into those without comprehensive plans and those with such plans, regardless of whether they were prepared under mandate. Furthermore, the quality of the plans can be assessed. Thus, the research design enabled us to explore another research question: Does the existence of a plan, and its quality, regardless of whether or not the plan is mandated by the state, lead to different or better development management strategies? Even within the eighty-eight communities of California, Florida, and North Carolina where planning is mandated, the research design allows exploration of the research question: Do specific mandate characteristics make a difference in either the quality and style of local planning or local development management strategies?

At the state level, the planning mandate programs and other state programs relevant to hazard mitigation are compared among the three states with planning mandates—California, Florida, and North Carolina (in the coastal zone)—and between the three states without mandates—Texas, Washington, and North Carolina (in the mountain region). In this approach, the sample size for the state-level analysis of state mandate context is six—three states or regions with comprehensive-planning mandates and three without. In another approach, the sample of state contexts consists of nineteen mandates: the three comprehensive-planning mandates of California, Florida, and North Carolina and sixteen other state mandates, spread among all five states, that address natural hazards.

Selection of States

We selected states for inclusion in this study on the basis of four considerations. First, we included both states with planning mandates and states without planning mandates. Second, variation is achieved in characteristics of planning mandates. Third, significant natural hazards exist both in states with mandates and in those without. Fourth, hazards, populations, and political cultures in the states without mandates are similar to those in one or more of the states with mandates.

California, Florida, and North Carolina each have well over a decade of experience with comprehensive-planning mandates regarding land use for local government jurisdictions. They provide variation in characteristics of such mandates (see chapter 1), which allows exploration of whether variation in mandate characteristics accounts for differences in local governmental planning and implementation. Although several other states employ planning mandates, we believe the sample of three states chosen is representative of state mandates and, therefore, that the findings can be generalized with a reasonable degree of confidence.

Washington, Texas, and the mountain region of North Carolina provide examples of areas without mandates (at the time fieldwork was done for the study) that are subject to natural hazards similar to those facing communities in the states with mandates. All six contexts, including the mountain region of North Carolina, have riverine flooding hazards, although such conditions are more severe in Florida and Texas than in the other three states. Washington is exposed to earthquake and landslide hazards, as is California. Texas is subject to coastal flooding and hurricanes, as are Florida and North Carolina. It should be noted that since the time fieldwork was completed for the study, Washington has enacted a planning mandate for its faster-growing local jurisdictions and Texas has introduced a coastal zone management program.

Selection of Local Governments

Local governments were selected at random from a list of all counties (and municipalities within them) that met four criteria:

1. The counties touch a coast, whether of an ocean or a large bay, estuary, or sound. This emphasis on coastal regions improves the comparability across the states, particularly since North Carolina's planning mandate is limited to its coastal region; but it makes generalization to non-coastal situations less valid. A municipality need not touch the coast; it only need be located in a county that touches the coast. An exception of the coastal county rule is made to include the sample of twenty-eight counties and municipalities in North Carolina's mountain region; this was the only way to get a comparison within the same state. The Texas sample contains no counties because counties there have no plan-making authority.
2. Municipalities and counties with 1990 census-estimated populations under twenty-five hundred were excluded to eliminate communities with limited governmental capacity (and to eliminate a strata of towns that would bias the sample by their large numbers) but still allow inclusion of a wide range of population sizes.
3. A few large local governments were excluded because, due to their complexity and uniqueness, they would be difficult to compare with the North Carolina coastal zone (which had no such cities) and to generalize to other places. Excluded on that basis were Los Angeles, San Diego, and San Francisco in California, Miami in Florida, and Seattle in Washington.
4. The municipality or county must be subject to a significant natural hazard. Very few communities are not.

Thirty communities were sampled at random in each state, with the exception of North Carolina. In that state, thirty communities are included

from the coastal region, where comprehensive land use planning is mandated, but there are also twenty-eight additional communities from the
mountain region, which is not covered by a planning mandate. In California
and the North Carolina mountain region cases, we were unable to obtain
responses from a full sample of thirty communities; the sample group includes twenty-eight communities in each. There are thirty-six counties and
140 municipalities in the sample. In states without mandates, fifty-two of
the eighty-eight communities have plans, and thirty-six have no plans. All
eighty-eight local governments in states with mandates have plans. Table A.1
gives a summary of the number of communities of various types.

Scope of Data Collected

Data were collected at both the state level and the local level. At the state
level, for plan-mandating states, information was gathered and organized as
a narrative on the historical evolution of relevant regulatory mandates in
each state. Data were also collected on the formal legislation and its requirements, sanctions, incentives, and other provisions. Finally, state officials
were interviewed about the resources and activities involved in implementing the planning mandate. In all states, including states without a comprehensive-planning mandate, information was compiled about the design of
hazards-related, single-purpose state mandates. Information included objectives, comprehensiveness of hazards covered, requirements for local use of
regulations, state actions to build local commitment and capacity, implementation complexity, and clarity of goals. Furthermore, state officials were
surveyed about the implementation of the program—level of funding,
staffing, implementation activities, and assessments of other aspects of implementation. Thus, data were collected on both the design of a mandate on
paper and the operation of the mandate in practice.

   At the local government level, each locality was surveyed concerning its
approach to natural hazards, each locality's plan was obtained (if it had one)
and systematically evaluated, and interviews were conducted with the planner about planning and development management.

State-Level Data Sources and Collection Methods

The state-level data effort applies to the three comprehensive-planning
mandates in California, Florida, and the North Carolina coastal region and

TABLE A.1

Summary of Local Government Sample Characteristics

Characteristic	Comprehensive-Planning and Single-Purpose Mandates			Single-Purpose Mandates Only		
	Calif.	Fla.	N.C. (coastal region)	Tex.	Wash.	N.C. (mountain region)
Number of local governments	28	30	30	30	30	28
Counties	1	3	14	0	6	12
Municipalities	27	27	16	30	24	16
Number subject to particular hazards						
Hurricane or coastal flooding	5	30	30	14	7	0
Riverine flooding	20	30	30	28	30	27
Earthquake	28	2	0	2	25	8
Landslide	20	2	0	0	26	16
Number with general plans	28	30	30	14	29	9
Median 1990 population						
Counties	340,421	211,707	21,455	——	108,851	36,894
Municipalities	41,333	13,024	4,027	10,443	6,968	3,977

to sixteen other state-level single-purpose mandates spread across the five states in the study. There were three approaches to collecting and describing data about the nineteen mandates.

In the first approach, the research team described the comprehensive-planning mandates in California, Florida, and North Carolina. The description included a history of their adoption and implementation and an analysis of factors that explained the choice of the particular mandate approach in each state. It also described the other sixteen single-purpose mandates across the five states. Finally, it examined the increasing use of state mandates over the past two decades, even in Texas and Washington. This first approach relied on the growing literature on state-level planning and management, as well as reports, other documents, and discussions with officials from the five states. This approach yielded a relatively independent description and analysis of the state mandates, reported in chapters 1 through 5, and allows for insights and a certain richness of understanding not possible under the second and third approaches to data collection.

The second and third approaches to data collection are more systematic and social-scientific, and they are combined in a statistical analysis (see chapter 6). In the second approach to data collection, mandate designs were characterized by coding key attributes of the relevant statutes and their associated administrative regulations. For each mandate, this entailed checking for the presence or absence of a series of prospective mandate provisions and characterizing mandate complexity, goal clarity, and the extent of system change according to a series of rating scales. As a check on the face validity of the mandate ratings, members of the study team from each state, who were familiar with their respective state's mandate provisions, reviewed the raw data coding and resultant rankings of mandates on key variables. This review led to one recombination of mandates (combining Texas dune and coastal mandates) and minor revisions in the coding of some mandate features to account for additional features not included in the original mandate coding. Checks on intercoder reliability are not possible, given the procedures followed for data collection. For the more subjective aspects entailing a rating of goal clarity of the mandates, a partial check on intercoder reliability is provided by a comparison of the senior investigator's ratings of the clarity of mandate goals with a research assistant's ratings. The mean Pearson correlation between the two ratings for the items that comprise this index is .79.

The third data source consisted of information about mandate implementation based on a questionnaire and interviews with program managers responsible for mandate implementation. Respondents were selected and interviews conducted, either in person or by phone, by members of the study team from each state (or region), who were knowledgeable about program specifics and who could provide appropriate probing of respondent characterizations of program implementation. Respondents were selected on the basis of ability to provide factual information about program implementation (e.g., funding and staffing levels) and assessments of program implementation. Typically, interviews consisted of a single respondent who managed or oversaw the program (i.e., the program manager or division director). Study team members found it necessary to interview either two or three respondents for five of the nineteen mandates. In these instances, assessments of program implementation were averaged across respondents for each mandate. The main weakness in these data consists of reliance upon single informants for many of the ratings of program implementation. This weakness is partially compensated by reliance on factual information for analysis of implementation effort and use of multiple items to construct scales with reasonably high internal consistency.

Many of the indexes in the study consist of summated-rating scales constructed from items contained in the coding of mandate design or the interviews about implementation (see Spector 1992). Items for each index were initially selected on the basis of face validity, with some items being dropped after data collection to improve internal consistency of the scale. Each item measuring mandate content was based on a series of three-point scales. Items measuring the quality of mandate goals and respondent characterizations of implementation were based on seven-point scales with descriptive anchors for each end point. The questionnaire items for each scale mixed positively and negatively worded items to force respondents to consider each item. The internal consistency of each summated scale was evaluated using Chronbach's alpha, for which the summated-rating scales have an average alpha of .76. Relevant details about the construction of each index are contained in table A.2. These state level variables are used in both the state-level comparisons and in the local-government-level analyses.

Local-Level Data Sources and Collection Methods

There were four data collection approaches at the local government level: an evaluation of the local comprehensive land use plan, a self-administered survey of local planners, supplementary interviews with local planners while picking up and checking the questionnaires, and collection of secondary data from the U.S. Census and other sources.

In the first of the four local-data collection efforts, comprehensive land use plans were obtained for all local governments in the sample that had such a plan. This included all communities in the three states with comprehensive-planning mandates and fourteen communities in Texas, twenty-nine communities in Washington, and nine in the North Carolina mountain region. Each plan was evaluated systematically, using plan-coding guidelines. Measures were constructed to assess three components of a plan—the information base, the goals, and the policy and action recommendations. In addition, five overall attributes of the plan were measured: comprehensiveness, integration of hazards issues with other issues, readability and legibility, interorganizational coordination, and specificity of implementation responsibility. The research teams in each state conducted internal plan-coding training sessions, compared coding results for identical plans to those

TABLE A.2

Measurement of State-Level Variables

Variable	Measurement	Source of Data
Mandate capacity-building features	Average rating[a] for: state-provided technical assistance regional or other technical assistance state-funded mapping or information state-provided education or training state funding for local personnel or equipment authorization for new local fees or taxing authority Higher scores indicate stronger mandate provisions for enhancing the capacity of local governments.	Coding of legislative provisions for individual state mandates
Mandate commitment-building features	Average rating[a] for: public awareness local governmental awareness incentive funding for local governments matching funding for local participation authorization of citizen suits to force compliance of local governments review or evaluation of local government regulations deadlines for local governmental action sanctions for local governmental failure to meet deadlines sanctions for local governmental failure to comply with mandate provisions state preemption of local authority Higher scores indicate stronger mandate provisions for enhancing the commitment of local governments	Coding of legislative provisions for individual state mandates
Mandate coercive features	Average rating[a] for: authorization of citizen suits deadlines for local government action sanctions for local governmental failure to meet deadlines	Coding of legislative provisions for individual state mandates

Variable	Measurement	Source of Data
	sanctions for local governmental failure to comply with mandate provisions state preemption of local authority Higher scores indicate stronger provisions for compelling compliance by local governments with state mandates	
Mandate goal clarity	Average rating[b] for: vagueness (vague to specific) complexity (complex to simple) directness (undirected to directed) specificity (broad to narrow) number of goals (many to few) Higher scores indicate mandates with clearer goals	Coding of legislative provisions for individual state mandates
Mandate implementation complexity	Sum of ratings[a] for: state organizational arrangements intergovernmental arrangements number of mandate goals number of state agencies involved frequency of mandated local actions deadlines for local action number of target groups Higher scores indicate greater complexity for implementation	Coding of legislative provisions for individual state mandates
Mandate incentive features	Average rating[a] for: state-provided technical assistance regional or other technical assistance state-funded education or training provisions for raising public awareness incentive funding for local governments Higher scores indicate greater use of incentives	Coding of legislative provisions for individual state mandates
Mandate mix of persuasive tools	Rating of coercive features minus rating of facilitative features (see above). Higher scores indicate greater emphasis on coercive features.	Coding of legislative provisions for individual state mandates
Single-purpose mandate strength	Sum of ratings of mandate commitment- and capacity-building features (see above) for single-purpose mandates in a given state. Higher scores indicate stronger policy prescription.	Interviews with state agency personnel

(continued)

TABLE A.2 (*continued*)

Variable	Measurement	Source of Data
State agency capacity	Average rating[b] for: adequacy of agency staffing for meeting hazard-related goals adequacy of agency expertise access to relevant local or regional governmental officials adequacy of agency authority for enforcing hazard-related provisions Higher scores indicate greater capacity of state agencies for carrying out state policy	Interviews with state agency personnel
State agency commitment	Average rating[b] for: agency endorsement of hazard-related goals importance of hazard-related goals relative to other mandate goals willingness of agency leadership to promote hazard-related goals status of individuals working on hazard-related activities extent of legislative support Higher scores indicate greater commitment of state agencies to mandate goals	Interviews with state agency personnel
State agency implementation effort	Percentage of staff time devoted to hazard-related activities times mandate expenditures per affected jurisdiction. Higher scores indicate greater implementation effort.	Interviews with state agency personnel
State agency implementation style	Average rating[b] for: use of sanctions (avoid to threaten) enforcement (bargaining to legal procedure) mode of communication (verbal to written) interpretation of administrative rules (flexible to strict adherence) form of compliance monitoring (goals and outcomes to process or deadline) Higher scores indicate more formal, legalistic implementation style	Interviews with state agency personnel

[a] Ratings on a three-point scale.

[b] Ratings on a seven-point scale.

of other teams, and adjusted procedures and guidelines until consistency was achieved across all five teams (states).

From the plan-coding effort, measures of plan quality and approach were constructed, including indexes of documentation of the hazards threat, goals relating to hazards mitigation specifically, and actions recommended to address natural hazards. These measures were made with respect to each type of hazard, as well as to hazards in general.

In the second of the four local-data collection efforts, local officials were contacted by phone and asked to participate in the study. They were then mailed a questionnaire designed to obtain data about the type and degree of hazards faced by the community, the attitudes of the community toward hazards and hazards mitigation, the planning agency and its operation, regulations and other measures used to mitigate risks from natural hazards, and the role of the comprehensive plan in hazard mitigation.

In the third of the four local-data collection efforts, the planner in each community was interviewed during a visit that included picking up and checking the questionnaire. The interview, averaging about an hour in length, addressed such issues as reasons for the lack of a plan (if the community had no plan) and its effect on the way the community addressed natural hazards, the people and issues involved in the plan-making process, the way the community determined how to respond to state mandates, the effect of state mandates and other programs on the way the local government addressed natural hazards, and the perceived effectiveness of land use planning and development management in the community. The responses were summarized on an interview guide form during and immediately following the interview and later condensed in a brief statement on each community. In the North Carolina mountain region, the interview was by telephone instead of in person. The interview visit also allowed interviewers to complete and collect the questionnaire and to obtain access to plan-related documents necessary to complete evaluation of the plan as well as to gain better understanding of the community and relevant natural hazards.

In the fourth approach to collecting data on local governments, data were obtained for each community from the U.S. Census and other sources about population size, population density, growth rate, geographic size of the jurisdiction, number of dwellings, median house value, housing occupancy rate, percent of dwellings that are seasonal, and number of repeat-loss properties under the National Flood Insurance Program.

Some of the variables used in the analyses reported in chapters 7 and 8 could not be measured from a single question or data source. Thus, they were constructed as indexes, using multiple questions or even several data sources. These variables are explained in table A.3.

TABLE A.3
Measurement of Local-Level Variables

Variable	Measurement	Source of Data
Plan quality	Average sum of ratings on a 3-point scale of the factual base for the plan for each of 10 items; ratings on a 2-point scale of the goals for each of 9 items; and ratings on a 3-point scale of policy recommendations for each of 24 items for each of four natural hazards (earthquakes, floods, hurricanes, and landslides). Sums for the fact basis, goals, and policy recommendations are standardized for the number of hazards present in a community. Factual items were coded 0 = not present; 1 = mentioned but not detailed; and 2 = mentioned and detailed. Goal items were coded 0 = not mentioned; 1 = mentioned. Policy items were coded 0 = not mentioned; 1 = suggested; 2 = mandatory. For a list of the items coded, see table, Components of Plan Quality, in chapter 7.	Coding of latest plan available in each community
Land use recommendations	Specific actions recommended in comprehensive plan. Index is summation of ratings on a 6-point scale for: prohibition or restriction of development in hazard-prone areas; density limits and lower density in hazard-prone areas; density bonuses in return for land dedication in hazard-prone areas; transfer of development rights for hazard mitigation; tax benefits for land dedication in hazard-prone areas	Coding of latest plan available in each community
Site design requirement recommendations	Specific actions recommended in comprehensive plan. Index is summation of ratings on a 5-point scale for: site plan review and special mitigation requirements for hazard-prone areas	Coding of latest plan available in each community

Variable	Measurement	Source of Data
	impact assessment as a basis for hazard mitigation for specific projects	
	mandatory setbacks from hazardous portions of sites	
	clustering to keep development away from hazard-prone parts of site	
Building standard recommendations	Specific actions recommended in comprehensive plan. Index is summation of ratings on a 4-point scale for:	Coding of latest plan available in each community
	special or stringent building code requirements in hazard-prone areas	
	required retrofitting of structures to meet current codes	
	low-interest loans to retrofit structures	
Knowledge enhancement recommendations	Specific actions recommended in comprehensive plan. Index is summation of ratings on an 8-point scale for:	Coding of latest plan available in each community
	public education campaign	
	early warning system	
	encouragement of earthquake or flood insurance	
	encouragement of voluntary disclosure of risks prior to sale of property	
	mandatory disclosure of risks prior to sale of property	
	technical assistance/workshops to reduce losses from hazards	
	signs posting boundaries of areas subject to natural hazards	
Infrastructure policy recommendations	Specific actions recommended in comprehensive plan. Index is summation of ratings on a 5-point scale for:	Coding of latest plan available in each community
	structural controls	
	capital improvements adjustments	
	retrofitting public infrastructure	
	addressing critical facilities	
Total number of development	Index is summation of techniques adopted on a 20-point scale for:	Planning agency questionnaire

(*continued*)

TABLE A.3 (*continued*)

Variable	Measurement	Source of Data
management techniques adopted	land use control techniques (0–5 techniques) site design requirement techniques (0–4 requirements) building standard techniques (0–3 techniques) knowledge enhancement techniques (0–7 techniques)	
Land use control techniques adopted	Index is summation of land use techniques adopted on a 6-point scale for: prohibition or restriction of development in hazard-prone areas density limits/lower density in hazard-prone areas density bonuses in return for land dedication in hazard-prone areas transfer of development rights for hazard mitigation tax benefits for land dedication in hazard prone areas	Planning agency questionnaire
Site design standards adopted	Index is summation of site design requirement techniques adopted on a 5-point scale for: site plan review and special mitigation requirements for hazard-prone areas impact assessment as a basis for hazard mitigation for specific projects mandatory setbacks from hazardous portions of sites clustering to keep development away from hazard-prone parts of site	Planning agency questionnaire
Building standard techniques adopted	Index is summation of building standard techniques adopted on a 4-point scale for: special or stringent building code requirements in hazard-prone areas required retrofitting of structures to meet current codes low-interest loans to retrofit structures	Planning agency questionnaire

Variable	Measurement	Source of Data
Knowledge enhancement techniques adopted	Index is summation of knowledge-enhancement techniques adopted on an 8-point scale for: public education campaign early warning system encouragement of earthquake or flood insurance encouragement of voluntary disclosure of risks prior to sale of property mandatory disclosure of risks prior to sale of property technical assistance and workshops to reduce losses from hazards signs posting boundaries of areas subject to natural hazards	Planning agency questionnaire
Number of structural protection techniques adopted	Index is summation of structural protection techniques adopted on a 10-point scale for: sea walls groins breakwaters tide gates levees channel improvements or diversions dams, reservoirs, and impoundments watershed treatment slope stabilization structures	Planning agency questionnaire
Planning staff commitment to hazard mitigation	Index is summation of ratings on an 8-point scale of planning agency commitment to managing natural hazards for: agency endorsement of hazard reduction goals director's willingness to promote these goals Higher scores indicate a greater degree of commitment	Planning agency questionnaire
Staff per capita	Number of planning agency staff members per 1,000 population in 1990	Planning agency questionnaire and U.S. Census
Elected official commitment to hazard mitigation	Ratings on a 5-point scale of elected officials' commitment to reducing the threat of losses from natural	Planning agency questionnaire

(continued)

TABLE A.3 (*continued*)

Variable	Measurement	Source of Data
	hazards over the past decade. Higher scores indicate a greater degree of commitment.	
Political demands for solutions	Index is summation of ratings on a 5-point scale of demands made over the past decade by four different interest groups for local government to address natural hazards. Each group coded as 0 = no involvement; 1 = requested information; 2 = sought action; 3 = attended meetings; 4 = served on committees. Items: business groups environmental groups neighborhood groups unaffiliated individuals	Planning agency questionnaire
Stakeholder knowledge of problem	Cumulative percentage of residents and developers on a scale of 0 to 180 (0 percent to 90 percent or more) who have a "good understanding" of threats posed by natural hazards.	Planning agency questionnaire
Previous natural disaster	Rating on a 5-point scale of seriousness of disasters declared eligible for federal disaster aid over the past two decades. Coded as 0 = no federally declared disaster; 1 = small impact (small area, short duration); 2 = moderate impact (small area with extensive damage, or large area with moderate damage); 3 = large impact (widespread devastation, lengthy reconstruction period), 4 = enormous impact (widespread and severe devastation with long term effects).	Planning agency questionnaire
Repetitively flooded property	Number of properties that have suffered flood damage eligible for flood insurance on two or more occasions.	National Flood Insurance Program data file
Demand for land in hazard area	Index is summation of ratings on a 6-point scale of demand for development of vacant land in four hazard-prone areas over the past decade.	Planning agency questionnaire

Variable	Measurement	Source of Data
	Each item coded as 0 = very low demand to 5 = very high demand. Items: 100-year floodplain coastal hazard area (V zones) earthquake fault or liquefaction zones slopes subject to landslides	
Size of hazard area	Cumulative percentage of jurisdiction located in each of four hazard areas. Items: 100-year floodplain coastal hazard area (V zones) earthquake fault or liquefaction zones slopes subject to landslides	Planning agency questionnaire
1990 population	Size of population in 1990	U.S. Census
Population growth from 1980 to 1990	Percentage increase in population between 1980 and 1990	U.S. Census
Population density	1990 population divided by land area of jurisdiction	U.S. Census
Wealth	Median home value of owner-occupied housing in 1990	U.S. Census

References

Advisory Commission on Intergovernmental Relations. 1984. *Regulatory Federalism: Policy, Process, Impact, and Reform.* Publication A-95. Washington, D.C.: Advisory Commission on Intergovernmental Relations.

Alexander, Ernest R. 1985. "After Rationality, What? A Review of Responses to Paradigm Breakdown." *Journal of the American Planning Association* 50, no. 1: 62–69.

————. 1992. *Approaches to Planning.* 2d ed. Philadelphia: Gordon and Breach.

Alexander, Ernest R., and Andreas Faludi. 1989. "Planning and Plan Implementation: Notes on Evaluation Criteria." *Environment and Planning B: Planning and Design* 16, no. 2: 127–40.

Allen, L. M. 1989. "Changing the Cultural Myth: Hunters and Gatherers on the Coast." In *Living on the Edge: Collected Essays on Coastal Texas,* ed. Stephen J. Curley. Galveston: Texas A & M University.

Altshuler, Alan. 1965. *The City Planning Process: A Political Analysis.* Ithaca: Cornell University Press.

Balch, G. 1980. "The Stick, the Carrot, and Other Strategies: A Theoretical Analysis of Government Intervention." In *Policy Implementation: Penalties or Incentives,* ed. J. Brigham and D. W. Brown. Beverly Hills, Calif.: Sage Publications.

Banfield, Edward C., and Martin Meyerson. 1955. *Politics, Planning, and the Public Interest: The Case of Public Housing in Chicago.* Glencoe, Ill.: Free Press.

Bardach, Eugene, and Robert A. Kagan. 1982. *Going by the Book: The Problem of Regulatory Unreasonableness.* Philadelphia: Temple University Press.

Bartley, Ernest R. 1973. "Status and Effectiveness of Land Development Regulations in Florida Today." In *Environmental Conference on Land Use.* Miami, Fla.: Environmental Land Management Study Committee.

Berke, Philip, and Timothy Beatley. 1992. *Planning for Earthquakes: Risk, Politics, and Policy.* Baltimore: Johns Hopkins University Press.

Black, Alan. 1968. "The Comprehensive Plan." In *Principles and Practice of Urban Planning,* ed. William Goodman and Erik Freund. Washington, D.C.: International City Management Association.

Blackwelder, Barry. 1972. "Water Resources Development." In *Nixon and the En-*

vironment: The Politics of Devastation, ed. James Raltilesberger. New York: Village Voice/Taurus Communications.

Bollens, Scott A. 1993. "Restructuring Land Use Governance." Journal of Planning Literature 7, no. 3: 211–26.

Bosselman, Fred, David A. Feurer, and Charles L. Siemon. 1976. The Permit Explosion: Coordination of the Proliferation. Washington, D.C.: Urban Land Institute.

Brower, David J., and Laurie G. Ballenger. 1991. Permit Compliance Assessment. Prepared for the Division of Coastal Management, North Carolina Department of Environment, Health, and Natural Resources. Chapel Hill: Center for Urban and Regional Studies, University of North Carolina.

Bryson, John M. 1978. "A Case Study in the Planning and Implementation of a Growth Management System." Planning and Administration 5, no. 2: 53–63.

———. 1991. "There Is No Substitute for an Empirical Defense of Planning and Planners." Journal of Planning Education and Research 10, no. 2: 164–65.

Burby, Raymond J. 1977. "Natural Environmental Issues in North Carolina." Paper prepared for the NCAIP Regional Hearing on Natural Environmental Issues, January 7, Appalachian State University, Boone, North Carolina.

———. 1979. Second Homes in North Carolina. Raleigh: Water Resources Research Institute, University of North Carolina.

Burby, Raymond J., and Steven P. French. 1981. "Coping with Floods: The Land Use Management Paradox." Journal of the American Planning Association 47, no. 3: 289–300.

Burby, Raymond J., and Steven P. French, with Beverly Cigler, Edward J. Kaiser, David H. Moreau, and Bruce Stiftel. 1985. Flood Plain Land Use Management: A National Assessment. Boulder, Colo.: Westview Press.

Carter, Luther. 1975. The Florida Experience: Land and Water Policy in a Growth State. Baltimore: Johns Hopkins University Press.

Catanese, Alan J. 1974. Planners and Local Politics: Impossible Dreams. Beverly Hills, Calif.: Sage Publications.

Caves, Roger W. 1992. Land Use Planning: The Ballot Box Revolution. Newbury Park, Calif.: Sage Publications.

Chapin, F. Stuart, Jr., and Edward J. Kaiser. 1979. Urban Land Use Planning. 3d ed. Urbana: University of Illinois Press.

Comerio, Mary C. 1992. "Impacts of the Los Angeles Retrofit Ordinance on Residential Buildings." Earthquake Spectra 8, no. 1: 79–94.

Connerly, Charles. 1990. "State Mandated Housing Plans: How Effective Are They? A Case Study of Florida's Growth Management Act Housing Element Requirement." Paper prepared for the annual meeting of the Association of Collegiate Schools of Planning, November 1–4, Austin, Texas.

Cook, Stuart. 1990. Seismic Hazards and Land Use Planning: A Review of California Practice. Berkeley: Center for Environmental Design Research, University of California.

Cornwall, Charles. 1990. Seismic Hazards and Environmental Impact Assessment:

A *Review of Current California Practice.* Berkeley: Center for Environmental Design Research, University of California.

Culliton, Thomas J., et al. 1990. *Fifty Years of Population Change along the Nation's Coast: 1960–2010.* Rockville, Md.: National Oceanic and Atmospheric Administration.

Curley, Stephen J. 1990. "Texas Coastal Plan: Analysis of a Failure." *Coastal Management* 18, no. 1: 1–14.

Dalton, Linda C. 1989. "The Limits of Regulation: Evidence from Local Plan Implementation in California." *Journal of the American Planning Association* 55, no. 2: 151–68.

DeGrove, John M. 1984. *Land Growth and Politics.* Chicago: American Planning Association Planners Press.

———. 1990. "The Politics of Planning a Growth Management System: The Key Ingredients for Success." *Carolina Planning* 16, no. 1: 26–34.

DeGrove, John M., and Westi Jo deHaven-Smith. 1987. "Resource Planning and Management Committees: A Tool for Intergovernmental Coordination and Conflict Resolution." In *Coastal Zone '87.* New York: American Society of Civil Engineers.

DeGrove, John M., with Deborah A. Miness. 1992. *The New Frontier for Land Policy: Planning and Growth Management in the States.* Cambridge, Mass.: Lincoln Institute of Land Policy.

DeGrove, John M., and Nancy E. Stroud. 1987. "State Land Planning and Regulation: Innovative Roles in the 1980s and Beyond." *Land Use Law and Zoning Digest* 39 (March): 3–8.

deHaven-Smith, Lance. 1984. "Regulatory Theory and State Land-Use Regulation: Implications from Florida's Experience with Growth Management." *Public Administration Review* 44 (October): 413–20.

Deyle, Robert E., and Richard A. Smith. 1994. *Storm Hazard Mitigation and Post-Storm Redevelopment Policies.* Tallahassee, Fla.: Department of Urban and Regional Planning, Florida State University.

Donnelley Marketing Information Service. 1987. *System Update Report.* Washington, D.C.: Federal Emergency Management Agency.

Etzioni, Amitai. 1961. "Organizational Control Structures." In *Handbook of Organizations,* ed. James March. Chicago: Rand McNally.

Faludi, Andreas. 1987. *A Decision-Centered View of Environmental Planning.* Oxford, U.K.: Pergamon Press.

Fischer, Michael L. 1985. "California's Coastal Program: Larger-than-Local Interests Built into Local Plans." *Journal of the American Planning Association* 51, no. 3: 312–21.

Fishman, Richard. 1978. "The State of Art in Local Planning." Appendix to chapter 5 in *Housing for All under Law,* ed. Richard Fishman. A Report of the American Bar Association, Advisory Committee on Housing and Urban Growth. Cambridge, Mass.: Ballinger.

Flood Insurance Producers National Committee. 1988. *FIPNC* 2, no. 3 (November).

Florida Department of Community Affairs. 1986. *A Coastal Barriers Resource Manual: Federal and State Program Highlights.* Fort Lauderdale, Fla.: Joint Center for Environmental and Urban Problems, Florida Atlantic University/Florida International University.

Florida Governor's Growth Management Transition Team Task Force. 1991. "Initial Report to the Governor." In *Florida Planning.* Tallahassee, Fla.: Florida Chapter of the American Planning Association.

Forester, John. 1989. *Planning in the Face of Power.* Berkeley: University of California Press.

Gade, Ole, and H. Daniel Stillwell. 1986. *North Carolina: People and Environment.* Boone, N.C.: GEO-APP.

Gale, Dennis E. 1992. "Eight State-Sponsored Growth Management Programs: A Comparative Analysis." *Journal of the American Planning Association* 58, no. 4: 425–39.

Godschalk, David R., David J. Brower, and Timothy Beatley. 1989. *Catastrophic Coastal Storms: Hazard Mitigation and Development Management.* Durham: Duke University Press.

Goggin, Malcolm L., Ann O'M. Bowman, James P. Lester, and Laurence J. O'Toole Jr. 1990. *Implementation Theory and Practice: Toward a Third Generation.* Glenview, Ill.: Scott, Foresman.

Gormley, William T., Jr. 1989. *Taming the Bureaucracy: Muscles, Prayers, and Other Strategies.* Princeton: Princeton University Press.

———. 1992. "Food Fights: Regulatory Enforcement in a Federal System." *Public Administration Review* 52 (May–June): 271–80.

Gruber, Judith E. 1987. *Controlling Bureaucracies: Dilemmas in Bureaucratic Governance.* Berkeley: University of California Press.

Haar, Charles M. 1955a. "In Accordance with a Comprehensive Plan." *Harvard Law Review* 68: 1154–75.

———. 1955b. "The Master Plan: An Impermanent Constitution." *Harvard Law Review* 68: 353–77.

Haskell, Elizabeth H. 1976. *Land Use Organizations in North Carolina.* Prepared for the North Carolina Land Policy Council. Raleigh: Land Policy Staff, Office of State Planning, Department of Administration, State of North Carolina.

Healy, Robert G. 1976. *Land Use and the States.* Baltimore: Johns Hopkins University Press.

Heath, Milton S. 1974. "A Legislative History of the Coastal Area Management Act." *North Carolina Law Review* 52, no. 2: 345–98.

Hedge, David M., Donald C. Menzel, and Mark A. Krause. 1989. "The Intergovernmental Milieu and Street-Level Implementation." *Social Science Quarterly* 70 (June): 285–99.

Hedge, David M., Donald C. Menzel, and George H. Williams. 1988. "Regulatory

Attitudes and Behavior: The Case of Surface Mining and Behavior." *Western Political Quarterly* 42 (June): 323–40.

Hollander, Elizabeth, Leslie Pollock, Jeffrey Recklinger, and Frank Beal. 1988. "General Development Plans." In *The Practice of Local Government Planning,* 2d ed., ed. Frank So and Judith Getzels. Washington, D.C.: International City Management Association.

Huber, Peter W. 1986. "The Bhopalization of American Tort Law." In *Hazards: Technology and Fairness,* Series on Technology and Social Priorities, National Academy of Engineering. Washington, D.C.: National Academy Press.

Innes, Judith E. 1993. "Implementing State Growth Management in the United States: Strategies for Coordination." In *Growth Management: The Planning Challenge of the 1990s,* ed. Jay M. Stein. Beverly Hills, Calif.: Sage Publications.

———. 1995. "Planning Theory's Emerging Paradigm: Communicative Action and Interactive Practice." *Journal of Planning Education and Research* 14, no. 3: 183–89.

Interagency Hazard Mitigation Team. 1992. *Interagency Hazard Mitigation Team Report in Response to the August 24, 1992, Disaster Declaration for the State of Florida, FEMA-955–Dr-FL, Hurricane Andrew.* Atlanta, Ga.: Federal Emergency Management Agency.

Jackson, Richard H. 1979. *Land Use in America.* New York: John Wiley and Sons.

Jennings, Michael D. 1989. "The Weak Link in Land Use Planning." *Journal of the American Planning Association* 55, no. 2: 206–8.

Kagan, Robert A. 1994. "Regulatory Enforcement." In *Handbook of Regulation and Administrative Law,* ed. David H. Rosenbloom and Richard D. Schwartz. New York: Marcel-Dekker.

Kaiser, Edward J., David R. Godschalk, and F. Stuart Chapin Jr. 1995. *Urban Land Use Planning.* 4th ed. Urbana: University of Illinois Press.

Kent, T. J. 1991. *The Urban General Plan.* Chicago: American Planning Association.

Knaap, Gerrit. 1992. "Evaluating State Land Use Programs: Structured Thoughts and Research Strategy." Paper prepared for the annual meeting of the Association of Collegiate Schools of Planning, October 29–November 1, Columbus, Ohio.

Kusler, Jon A. 1980. *Regulating Sensitive Lands.* Cambridge, Mass.: Ballinger.

Lindblom, Charles. 1959. "The Science of Muddling Through." *Public Administration Review* 19 (spring): 78–88.

Liner, Charles D. 1982. *An Analysis of the Coastal Area Management Act Erosion Rate Setback Regulation.* Chapel Hill: Institute of Government, University of North Carolina.

Linowes, R. Robert, and Don T. Allensworth. 1975. *The States and Land Use Control.* New York: Praeger.

Logan, John R., and Harvey L. Molotch. 1987. *Urban Fortunes: The Political Economy of Place.* Berkeley: University of California Press.

Louthain, Jerry. 1994. "Profile: Floodplain Management in Washington State." *News and Views* (newsletter of the Association of State Floodplain Managers) (April): 4–5.

Lovell, Catherine, and Charles Tobin. 1981. "The Mandate Issue." *Public Administration Review* 41 (May–June): 318–31.

L. R. Johnston Associates. 1992. *Floodplain Management in the United States: An Assessment Report*. Vol. 2, *Full Report*. Washington, D.C.: U.S. Government Printing Office.

Mandelker, Daniel R. 1989. "The Quiet Revolution—Success and Failure." *Journal of the American Planning Association* 55, no. 2: 204–5.

May, Peter J. 1991. "Reconsidering Policy Design: Policies and Publics." *Journal of Public Policy* 11, no. 2: 187–206.

———. 1993. "Mandate Design and Implementation: Enhancing Implementation Efforts and Shaping Regulatory Styles." *Journal of Policy Analysis and Management* 12, no. 4: 634–63.

May, Peter J., and Walter Williams. 1986. *Disaster Policy Implementation: Managing Programs under Shared Governance*. New York: Plenum Press.

Mazmanian, Daniel A., and Paul A. Sabatier. 1983. *Implementation and Public Policy*. Glenview, Ill.: Scott, Foresman.

McCluney, William R. 1971. *The Environmental Destruction of South Florida*. Miami, Fla.: University of Miami Press.

Mead, Susan. 1993. "This Is Texas, Not California or Florida." In *State and Regional Comprehensive Planning: Implementing New Methods for Growth Management*, ed. Peter A. Buchsbaum and Larry J. Smith. Chicago, Ill.: American Bar Association.

Mintier, J. Laurence, and Peter Arne Stromberg. 1983. "Seismic Safety at the Local Level: Does Planning Make a Difference?" *California Geology* 36, no. 7: 148–54.

National Commission on Urban Problems. 1968. *Building the American City*. Report to the Congress and the President of the United States. Washington, D.C.: U.S. Government Printing Office.

Netter, Edith, and Daniel Mandelker. 1981. "Mandatory Comprehensive Planning: Perspectives from Three States." In *Land Use Law: Issues for the Eighties*, ed. Edith Netter. Washington, D.C.: American Planning Association Planners Press.

North Carolina Land Policy Council. 1976. *Final Report*. Raleigh: Department of Administration, State of North Carolina.

North Carolina Marine Science Council. 1972. *North Carolina's Coastal Resources*. Preliminary Planning Report for Marine and Coastal Resource Development in North Carolina. Raleigh: Department of Administration, State of North Carolina.

Nosson, Linda Lawrence, Anthony Quamar, and Gerald W. Thorsen. 1988. *Washington State Earthquake Hazards*. Information Circular 85. Olympia: Department of Natural Resources, Division of Geology and Earth Resources, State of Washington.

Olshansky, Robert B. 1993. "The California Environmental Quality Act and Local Planning." *Planning and Public Policy* 16, no. 2: 1–4.

Owens, David W. 1985. "Coastal Management in North Carolina: Building a Regional Consensus." *Journal of the American Planning Association* 51, no. 3: 322–29.

Palm, Risa. 1981. *Real Estate Agents and Special Studies Zones Disclosure.* Boulder: Institute of Behavioral Science, University of Colorado.

Paterson, Robert G. 1988. "Strengthening Florida Floodplain Management: A Challenge to Local, Regional, and State Governments." *Environmental and Urban Issues* 15, no. 41: 12–17.

Pelham, Thomas G. 1979. *State Land-Use Planning and Regulation.* Lexington, Mass.: Lexington Books.

Pelham, Thomas G., William L. Hyde, and Robert Banks. 1985. "Managing Florida's Growth: Toward An Integrated State, Regional, and Local Comprehensive Planning Process." *Florida State University Law Review* 13, no. 3: 515–98.

Petak, William J., and Arthur A. Atkisson. 1982. *Natural Hazard Risk Assessment and Public Policy: Anticipating the Unexpected.* New York: Springer-Verlag.

Pitkin, Stephen. 1992. "Comprehensive Plan Format: A Key to Impacting Decision Making." *Environmental and Urban Issues* 19, no. 4: 8–10.

Pivo, Gary. 1993. "Is the Growth Management Act Working? A Survey of Resource Lands and Critical Areas Development Regulations." *University of Puget Sound Law Review* 16, no. 3: 1141–79.

Platt, Rutherford. 1987. *Regional Management of Metropolitan Floodplains.* Boulder: Institute of Behavioral Science, University of Colorado.

———. 1991. *Land Use Control: Geography, Law, and Public Policy.* Englewood Cliffs, N.J.: Prentice-Hall.

Popper, Frank. J. 1981. *The Politics of Land-Use Reform.* Madison: University of Wisconsin Press.

———. 1988. "Understanding American Land Use Regulation since 1970: A Revisionist Interpretation." *Journal of the American Planning Association* 54, no. 3: 91–301.

Powell, David L., Robert M. Rhodes, and Dan R. Stengle. 1995. "Florida's New Law to Protect Private Property Rights." *Environmental and Urban Issues* 23, no. 1: 10–19.

Reitherman, Robert. 1992. "The Effectiveness of Fault Zone Regulations in California." *Earthquake Spectra* 8, no. 1: 57–77.

Rossi, Peter H., James D. Wright, and Eleanor Weber-Burdin. 1982. *Natural Hazards and Public Choice: The State and Local Politics of Hazard Mitigation.* New York: Academic Press.

Rowe, Peter. 1978. *Principles for Local Environmental Management.* Cambridge, Mass.: Ballinger.

Sager, Tore. 1990. *Communicate or Calculate: Planning Theory and Social Science Concepts in a Contingency Perspective.* Stockholm: Nordplan.

Salkin, Patricia. 1993. "Growth Management Statutes: A National Overview." Albany School of Law, Albany, N.Y.

Schoenbaum, Thomas J. 1974. "The Management of Land and Water Use in the Coastal Zone: A New Law Is Enacted in North Carolina." *North Carolina Law Review* 53, no. 2: 275–302.

Scholz, John T. 1991. "Cooperative Regulatory Enforcement and the Politics of Administrative Effectiveness." *American Political Science Review* 85 (March): 115–36.

———. 1994. "Managing Regulatory Enforcement in the United States." In *Handbook of Regulation and Administrative Law,* ed. David H. Rosenbloom and Richard D. Schwartz. New York: Marcel Dekker.

Scholz, John T., and Feng Heng Wei. 1986. "Regulatory Enforcement in a Federalist System." *American Political Science Review* 80 (December): 1249–70.

Settle, Richard L. 1983. *Washington Land Use and Environmental Law and Practice.* Seattle, Wash.: Butterworth Legal Publications.

Simon, Herbert A. 1957. *Models of Man, Social and Rational.* New York: John Wiley and Sons.

Smith, Larry J. 1993. "Planning for Growth, Washington Style." In *State and Regional Comprehensive Planning: Implementing New Methods for Growth Management,* ed. Peter A. Buchsbaum and Larry J. Smith. Chicago, Ill.: American Bar Association.

Spector, Paul E. 1992. *Summated Rating Scale Construction, Quantitative Applications in the Social Sciences.* Monograph 82. Newbury Park, Calif.: Sage Publications.

Stone, Catherine E., and Philip A. Seymour. 1993. "California Land-Use Planning Law: State Preemption and Local Control." In *State and Regional Comprehensive Planning: Implementing New Methods for Growth Management,* ed. Peter A. Buchsbaum and Larry J. Smith. Chicago, Ill.: American Bar Association.

Talen, Emily. 1996. "Do Plans Get Implemented? A Review of Evaluation in Planning." *Journal of Planning Literature* 10, no. 3: 249–59.

Texas General Land Office. 1990. *Texas Coastal Management Plan.* Austin: Texas General Land Office.

Tilling, Robert I. 1987. *Eruptions of Mount St. Helens: Past, Present, and Future.* U.S. Geological Survey. Washington, D.C.: U.S. Government Printing Office.

Van Meter, Donald S., and Carl E. Van Horn. 1975. "The Policy Implementation Process: A Conceptual Framework." *Administration and Society* 6 (February): 445–88.

Wallis, Allan D. 1993. "Growth Management in Florida." Working Papers Series. Cambridge, Mass.: Lincoln Institute of Land Policy.

Washington Department of Ecology. 1988. *Floodplain Management Handbook for*

Local Administrators. Publication 88-10. Olympia: Department of Ecology, State of Washington.

Washington State Building Code Council. 1989. *A Study of Code Enforcement in Washington State: Report to the Governor and Washington State Legislature.* Olympia: Department of Community Development, State of Washington.

Washington State Land Planning Commission. 1973. *Land Planning for Our Future.* Olympia: Land Planning Commission, State of Washington.

Wilson, James Q. 1989. *Bureaucracy: What Government Agencies Do and Why They Do It.* New York: Basic Books.

Wood, Albert L. 1974. *Deviant Behavior and Control Strategies.* Lexington, Mass.: Lexington Books.

Wyner, Alan J., and Dean E. Mann. 1983. "Seismic Safety Policy in California: Local Governments and Earthquakes." Department of Political Science, University of California, Santa Barbara.

Index

Simon, Herbert, 13
Single-purpose mandates. *See* Mandates, single-purpose
Site design: and commitment of planning staff, 129; and constituency demands, 130, 131; and development management, 116, 122–23, 124n; effects of plan quality on, 128; and hazard mitigation, 122; and plan implementation, 119; in research design, 166, 168; and single-purpose mandates, 126
Smith, Richard, 59
Spellman, John, 74
Standard City Planning Enabling Act (1928), 12
Standards, development, 12. *See also* Building standards; Development management
Standard Zoning Act (1922), 12
State agencies: Florida's, 83; implementation effort of, 92–94, 140; implementation styles of, 16, 80, 85–86, 87, 88, 138; legislation governing, 93; and local governments, 86–92; and local officials, 150; priority setting of, 92; in research design, 23, 164; role of, 15; and state mandates, 79
State and Regional Planning Act (1984), Florida's, 52–53
State Comprehensive Planning Act (1985), Florida's, 53
State Environmental Policy Act (SEPA), Washington's, 74–75
State Lands Act (1959), North Carolina's, 40
Statutory coherence, 96, 98, 143
Stillwell, Dan, 39
Stream channelization, 114–15
Stromberg, Peter, 31
Structural protection: and commitment of planning staff, 129; and constituency demands, 130, 131; and development management, 116, 123, 125n; effects of plan quality on, 128; in research design, 169; and single-purpose mandates, 126. *See also* Building standards; Hazards, natural

Sunset laws, North Carolina's, 45
Systat statistical package, 89n, 94n

Technical assistance, 82; in Florida, 56; in North Carolina, 42; and plan quality, 108; and state mandates, 17
Texas: coastal development in, 66–67, 68; comprehensive-planning mandates of, 97, 105; development management in, 76; flood insurance claims in, 67; increasing use of state mandates in, 159; information strategies in, 127; local governments in, 159; local planning response in, 67–68, 139; natural hazards in, 156–57; plan implementation in, 120; plan quality of, 106; in research design, 156, 159; single-purpose mandates in, 70–71, 83–84
Texas Coastal Management Plan for Beach Access Preservation and Enhancement, Dune Protection, and Coastal Erosion Act (1991), 69
Texas General Land Office, Coastal Division of, 71
Tidewater, N.C., managing land use in, 40–42

Uniform Building Code, California's, 33–34
Unreinforced Masonry Law (1986), California's, 34–35
Urban development, and fragile ecology, 49. *See also* Development management
Urban growth, political costs of limiting, 100

Vermont: comprehensive-planning mandates of, 5, 10, 11; consistency requirements in, 9; land management in, 1, 2; persuasive measures used in, 10
Vertical consistency, 8, 43, 53, 137. *See also* Consistency requirements
Virginia, land use issues in, 45
Volcanic hazards, in Washington state, 72

About the Authors

RAYMOND J. BURBY is DeBlois Chair of Urban and Public Affairs and Professor of Urban and Regional Planning in the College of Urban and Public Affairs at the University of New Orleans.

PETER J. MAY is Professor of Political Science at the University of Washington.

PHILIP R. BERKE is Associate Professor of City and Regional Planning at the University of North Carolina at Chapel Hill.

LINDA C. DALTON is Professor of City and Regional Planning at California Polytechnic State University, San Luis Obispo.

STEVEN P. FRENCH is Professor and Director of the City Planning Program at the Georgia Institute of Technology.

EDWARD J. KAISER is Professor and Chair of the Department of City and Regional Planning at the University of North Carolina at Chapel Hill.

Library of Congress Cataloging-in-Publication Data

Burby, Raymond J., 1942–
    Making governments plan : state experiments in managing land use /
Raymond J. Burby and Peter J. May with Philip R. Berke . . . [et al.].
        p.   cm.
    "Published in cooperation with the Center for American Places, Harrisonburg,
Virginia"—Copr. p.
    Includes bibliographical references and index.
    ISBN 0-8018-5623-X (alk. paper)
    1. Land use—United States—States—Planning.   2. Land use—
Government policy—United States—States—Case studies.   I. May, Peter J.
II. Center for American Places (Harrisonburg, Va.)   III. Title.
HD205.B87   1997
333.73'17'0973—dc21   97-2189
                                                                                    CIP